THE ASSESSMENT OF
EARLY CHILD DEVELOPMENT

THE

ASSESSMENT

OF

EARLY CHILD

DEVELOPMENT

DOROTHY FLAPAN
and
PETER B. NEUBAUER

Jason Aronson   New York

ISBN: 0-87668-145-3

Library of Congress Catalog Number: 74-6946

Contents

THE ASSESSMENT OF
EARLY CHILD DEVELOPMENT

Chapter 1
Need for a Short
Assessment Outline

Theoretical writings and recent research have alerted professionals and nonprofessionals alike to the importance of the effect that the early years of childhood exert on later development. In some cases, serious pathology in the first years may slow development or distort it in some way. In other cases, the child entering nursery school is already so limited by his earlier experiences that he is unable to respond to, or benefit from, the enriching environment provided within the school setting — and learning does not take place.

Consequently, more and more interest has been shown in the possibility that some of the problems and difficulties of children can be recognized and evaluated in the initial stages and can thus be successfully handled at that time.

In this connection, there has been increasing awareness of the need for a way of assessing young children that would facilitate decisions about the appropriate services to be provided. By identifying at as early an age as possible the children who need, and can benefit from, specific services and attention, there is more likelihood that such children will receive the prescribed help at that time, whether in an educational setting, a mental health facility, or a community agency. At the least, there can be gross differentiation between children in the community who need to be referred to a treatment resource for serious pathology and children who simply need some type of modification in their school program, such as minimizing the stresses and strains that might contribute to problems, or providing conditions that might in some way maximize optimal development.

Throughout the United States, programs have been and are being developed to investigate the wide variety of services that can be offered for children from infancy on — programs within the areas of physical health, mental health, and education.

Day-care centers, public health agencies, and community health programs, as well as nursery schools and social agencies, are channels for early interaction with children, early assessment of them, and identification of those who may need more attention or some type of special attention. Although these various institutions in themselves are settings in which the child must cope with many kinds of challenging situations, the institutions can simultaneously provide emotional support and help.

With the range of services that are currently available, decisions can be made as to the specific type of environment best suited for a particular child. In addition, plans can be formulated to modify, eliminate, or delay certain experiences that might at a given time create difficulties for the child or add to his current problems; and specific experiences can be provided that would enhance his special skills or abilities and build on his strengths and competences.

Services have been expanded to reach more children than ever before, ranging from the normal to the abnormal and including children from a wider range of sociocultural as well as socioeconomic backgrounds.

Because a large proportion of these children were found to show difficulties in their learning capacities, cognition and cognitive development have been emphasized. For example, programs have been instituted to teach children basic mathematical and scientific concepts, even at the nursery-school and kindergarten levels. Techniques have been worked out to develop reading readiness; increase vocabulary; teach children how to manipulate symbols, how to solve complicated intellectual problems, and how to improve their performances on standard intelligence tests. And much effort has gone into devising ways to arouse the child's curiosity, motivate him, and encourage him to learn.

However, to prepare children for their future, it is necessary to consider and take responsibility for more than just cognitive development. Children need more than just the skills or facts that were considered sufficient in the past. If a child is anxious or troubled or experiencing some inner conflict, he may not be able to respond to the teacher's challenges or to the attractive new equipment or to the exciting new techniques.

It has become apparent that many young children do have inner anxieties and unresolved conflicts that interfere with their functioning and with their further development. Thus, it is necessary for those who are in daily, regular contact with young children to broaden their own perspectives if they are to contribute to the fullest development of the children's potentialities.

More and more people are in contact with children during the early years. The number of professionals in the fields of day care, early childhood education, and community health has increased. At the same time, there has been an increasing use of paraprofessionals in all these areas. These people — professionals and paraprofessionals — are in a crucial position not only to "screen" young children who need various types of help but to manipulate the environment in many ways to maximize each child's development.

This does not mean that the day-care workers, teachers, or community health specialists are expected to become therapists for the children or to become family counselors. However, they may help a child in other ways. They may, for example, facilitate the child's separation from his mother, aid him to establish relationships with peers, allow him to learn to assert himself. But along with their direct work with the children in these ways, and in addition to it, they can make a valuable contribution by becoming sensitized to the signs of developing problems, inner conflict, and anxiety, so that children who need it will receive the required help.

The use of consultants, school psychologists, and school social workers is growing. These people are of service to the day-care workers, teachers, and community health specialists by conferring with them, seeing children for further intensive study, or referring children to one of the mental health resources in the community for further assessment and/or therapy.

However, all this requires that persons having steady contact with young children be aware of the kinds of behavior to look at in assessing children and be able to present their observations in a form usable by clinical consultants and other educators. Individuals trained in education or community health often recognize intuitively that the child is having some difficulties or problems, that "something is not right," but there is then the task of communicating this intuition to others in a standardized, systematic form.

A large number of the people in ongoing in-service training programs for nursery school teachers, day-care workers, and community health specialists, as well as students in some of the innovative educational programs at community colleges and graduate schools, have voiced a need for an easy-to-use, standardized, reliable instrument to function as an initial, gross, "screening" device in nonclinical settings. They have expressed their desire for something that will focus their attention more on specific behaviors and problems. Attempting to look at these behaviors and to assess a child in this way would then help in choosing the kind of assistance need — in deciding, for example, among provision of a one-to-one relationship with an adult, reinforcement of ego controls, or practice in a specific skill.

Many developmental outlines and developmental profiles, such as the one by Anna Freud, try to take in as many variables and areas as can be observed and to integrate these in order to achieve an assessment of the child. Such a profile is quite thorough and should lead to a full developmental picture. However, it takes a great deal of knowledge about children's development and early pathology and a great deal of clinical training before it can validly be used. In addition, much time is required to produce such an assessment. Thus, this type of profile would not be practicable for use with the nonclinical professionals and paraprofessionals who are most urgently in need of assessment techniques today.

On the other hand, there has been much effort at developing rating forms, which range from problem checklists to trait and personality-structure assessment. Although these can be filled out in a relatively short time, most of them look specifically at pathological behavior or else concentrate on cognitive development.

Chapter 2
Study of Early
Child Development

To explore the problem of systematically studying early child development with the goal of evolving a short assessment procedure, the Child Development Center received a grant of money from The Grant Foundation. Research was designed with the aim of developing a short outline that would emphasize a few essential features of development and that would permit a preliminary grouping of children, rather than a complete assessment. Only the minimum necessary information was to be included. In this way, gross judgments, or "sophisticated estimates," could be made about the children; and from such an initial assessment, children could then be "screened" for further intensive study whenever it was deemed advisable.

The Child Development Center was in a favorable position to work on the task of evolving an assessment instrument that would be acceptable to, and usable by, a variety of groups of clinical and nonclinical professionals. It had available a staff of clinicians with many years of experience both in diagnosing young children who were having various difficulties (and who needed treatment) and in providing a variety of modalities of help through a therapeutic nursery school, an outpatient clinic for young children and their parents, group counseling programs with mothers, and through consultation arrangements with neighborhood schools and agencies.

A further advantage was the Child Development Center's long tradition of an interprofessional approach. Having psychiatrists, psychologists, social workers, and teachers who were accustomed to working together meant that many different perspectives and different emphases could be brought to bear on the task.

The ultimate goal was to use clinical knowledge and experience in a way that would make a contribution to those who were in regular daily contact with young children, to bridge the separation between clinicians and nonclinicians so that the fruits of clinical experience could be carried over to and benefit the larger community.

At the outset of the study, assessment was conceived of in terms of health/pathology. However, the approach soon shifted to that of assessing developmental progression rather than health.[1] After an exploratory study of a sample of nursery school children and after many months devoted to seminars, workshops, and discussions of this problem, it was decided that development represents the major task of childhood and that the capacity to maintain development could serve as a yardstick by which to assess children and differentiate among them.

At that time, this was a novel approach in evaluating children, but one which we thought had several positive aspects. Developmental progression can be more easily defined and agreed upon than can "health" or "normality," and thus the developmental approach seemed to offer more potential for establishing validity and reliability than did the health approach. Also, the developmental approach seems to be more easily used by and more useful to nonclinicians.

Another consideration in preferring the developmental rather than the health approach, however, is that what is seen at a given moment as unhealthy may in the long run be of less significance for the child. Time itself often brings

[1]For an explanation of this, see Dorothy Flapan and Peter B. Neubauer, "Issues in Assessing Development," *Journal of the American Academy of Child Psychiatry*, 9:669–687, 1970.

changes. Thus, some disorders have much significance in terms of the child's current functioning, but little significance in long-range terms.

On the other hand, development may proceed in spurts and stops, or there may be periodic regression followed by progression; a cross-sectional assessment of health may thus give an inaccurate picture of the child. Development is ongoing and continuous. This implies movement and evaluation only over an extended period of time. The developmental approach studies the child from birth to the moment of evaluation.

This type of assessment does not try to make a statement according to some diagnosis based on a symptom evaluation. Rather, it is interested to see whether any disorders or symptoms have interfered with further development and how the processes of development in turn have affected the symptoms of children. It tries to get away from field-oriented and field-specific diagnostic categories and to take into account the moving and changing characteristics of children.

Formulation of the Research Study

When the research study was originally formulated at the Child Development Center, a plan involving four steps was set forth. First, the methods usually used in diagnosing children in a clinical setting were to be applied to a sample of nonclinical children who were attending nursery schools in the community. In carrying out this part of the study, an attempt was to be made to set up an outline guide that would result in as comprehensive and complete an assessment of each child as was possible.

Next, these nonclinical children were to be followed over a period of several years, with annual assessment of each child, in order to observe which children developed serious problems or disturbances and what types of problems the children developed. Our focus was to be primarily on the children. We did not, in this study, plan to focus on the parents' handling of the children.

Third, an analysis was to be made to determine which aspects of development and which specific behaviors of the children differentiated between groups of children.

Then, as a final step, these behaviors and aspects of development were to be incorporated as items within a short form practicable for use by nonclinicians, such as nursery school teachers, public health nurses and child care workers.

Data Gathering

The research project began with the study of a large sample of middle-class children attending a private nursery school in the community, one at which the parents paid a moderate tuition. All the parents were college graduates and many had graduate degrees. These fathers and mothers were, for the most part, active in such professions as law, medicine, engineering, and the arts; or they were business executives. Later, the study was extended to include a sample of children of working-class background, who were on scholarships in private nursery schools or were in nursery schools in various community centers or settlement houses. Practically all the parents of these children were high-school graduates and had no college. They were primarily policemen, firemen, bus drivers, postal workers, and blue-collar workers.

In both samples of children, those who were judged to be retarded, schizophrenic, or organically brain damaged, as well as those who were currently receiving psychotherapy, were excluded. Thus, the study had a select group of "normal" children, considered by their parents and their teachers to be functioning more or less adequately at home and in the nursery school situation.

These children were seen initially at about 3–4 years of age, then at 4–5, and finally at 5–6.

The usual clinical method of data gathering was followed. This included semistructured interviews with each of the children, their parents, and their teachers; observation of the children in the school setting; and administration of a battery of psychological tests. The interviews and observations were done by psychiatrists, psychologists, and psychiatric social workers,[2] all of whom followed an extensive interview guide based on psychoanalytic formulations. In addition, psychological examiners[3] administered the Stanford Binet Intelligence test, the Rorschach ink blots, the Children's Apperception Test, and a figure-drawing test.

The clinician who did the interviewing and observing made an assessment of the child's development on the basis of each source of information; the psychological examiner made a separate assessment of the child's development, based on the psychological tests administered; and then the clinician wrote a dynamic summary integrating the material from all the interviews and observations with the information from the psychological tests and made a final, overall assessment of the child's development based on integration of all the information available.

This complete clinical data gathering, work-up, and assessment required about twenty-five hours for each child each year.

Groupings of the Children

The staff used this complete work-up of clinical material as a basis for differentiating between groups of children. After trying several different ways of grouping the children, the following groupings were evolved.[4] It

[2]Interviewers included R. Barazani, Ph.D.; B. Cramer, M.D.; L. Dimitrovsky, Ph.D.; D. Flapan, Ph.D.; N. Frankel, M.D.; L. Friedberger, Ph.D.; T. Gardian, M.S.W.; R. Geller, Ph.D.; G. Gunn, M.A.; P. Gunther, M.A.; J. Hart, M.A.; J. Kuppersmith, Ph.D.; H. Rahtz, M.S.W.; L. Sabot, M.D.; A. Sax, M.D.; M. Stein, M.D.; A. Tucker, Ph.D.

[3]Psychological examiners included S. Farber, Ph.D.; L. Friedberger, Ph.D.; L. Gruenthal; J. Kuppersmith, Ph.D.; A. Tucker, Ph.D.

[4]These findings appear in Dorothy Flapan and Peter B. Neubauer, "Developmental Groupings of Pre-School Children," *The Israel Annals of Psychiatry and Related Disciplines,* 10:52-70, 1972.

should be noted that the distance between Group 1a and Group 1b is not equal to the distance between Group 2 and Group 3. These are not groups differentiated quantitatively, but the numbers are just a way of setting up different groups, which could easily be called A^1, A^2, B, C, instead of 1a, 1b, 2, 3.

Group 1. Progression in development has been maintained.
a. Without accompanying pathology,
b. With significant accompanying pathological features.

Group 2. Progression in development has been interfered with in significant areas.

Group 3. Progression in development *had* been interfered with in significant areas, but is again proceeding.

In the research study, we found that it was possible to differentiate between the four groupings of children and to get agreement between clinicians as to these assessments of the children. In other words, it was possible (1) to differentiate children who maintained development from children who showed interference with development in significant areas, and (2) to differentiate children with significant pathology from children with minimal pathology.[5]

[5]Dorothy Flapan and Peter B. Neubauer, "Developmental Groupings of Pre-School Children," *The Israel Annals of Psychiatry and Related Disciplines*, 10:52-70, 1972.

Chapter 3
Aspects of Development —
Social Development and
Emotional Development

In attempting to assess developmental progression in young children, it was important to decide which aspects of development were most significant. Before systematic data-gathering was started, therefore, several preliminary questions had to be answered. What specifically was to be evaluated? How was it to be evaluated? Which general areas of development and which behaviors within each area were to be examined? How feasible was it to get the information desired?

To arrive at the final short assessment outline, it was necessary first to use a long form and then to reduce from this. Consequently, there was a continuous reduction over many years of data gathering (see Appendix A). The form that finally resulted was based on ten years of research with children and with various formats. Some of the items, of course, are similar to items in other ratings or checklists. However, the total integration of all items into one overall picture reflects our own orientation and analysis.

A developmental approach, looking at many developmental lines at the same time, had been discussed for some time by Anna Freud. She emphasized the assessment of the total personality rather than just one isolated aspect. Our work was greatly influenced by Miss

Freud, though it was also affected by ideas suggested by other writers and by the ideas of our own research staff.[1]

Based on a theoretical model derived from psychoanalytic developmental psychology, it was assumed that development proceeds in stages, or phases. At each phase the child is expected to show certain developmental landmarks and certain kinds of behavior, as well as to experience certain concerns, anxieties, and conflicts. In his social milieu, the child encounters certain expectations and conditions with which he must cope, has certain experiences which may affect his development, and develops certain characteristics, skills, and behaviors as he matures, which can be taken as indices of his developmental progression.

In the research study at the Child Development Center, it was found that conflicts or difficulties in the sample of nonclinical children were most likely to show up in the child's relationships with others and/or in the expression or lack of expression of feelings. On the other hand, even though such a child was having various difficulties, conflicts, or problems, he could more or less maintain the same IQ and continue intellectual functioning in the school situation. In the staff discussions about the individual nonclinical children during the several years of clinical data gathering and data analysis, it was found that the child's relationships with other people were usually mentioned first and most frequently in making an assessment of the child's developmental progression, and that the emotions or feelings were also given much emphasis in these discussions. Thus, it was concluded that these were both essential aspects of development and were to be included in an assessment outline.

Because the study was undertaken with a psychoanalytic developmental framework, it was also considered important to look at ego development, phase development (which included the libidinal phases of

---

[1]Such writers as E.H. Erikson, L.B. Murphy, J.W. Macfarlane, S. Chess, and A. Thomas.

development, the aggressive drive, and various disorders, symptoms, and problems), and superego development (which included self-esteem and the ego-ideal). Based on the experiences of attempting to assess the children over many years, it was decided that each of these aspects of development has a unique role in the overall assessment of the child's developmental progression.

For each of the five aspects of development included, the study was interested primarily in selecting items that would be relevant as possible indices of overall developmental progression, as well as indices of that particular aspect. The concern was more with developmental progression in general than with a specific age-norm for a given item. There was an attempt to state, in broad general terms, the expected development within each given area. Following this, one of the problems was to select items for which there were overt behavioral references. This involved working to translate theoretical concepts and propositions into observable behaviors, from which inferences could be made — that is, to spell out specific kinds of behaviors that would be included within each area.

In addition to making inferences from observed behavior, however, it was also considered necessary to look at absences of behaviors, traits, and trends usually expected and taken for granted as part of the developmental progression. For example, the absence of any assertiveness or the absence of a show of feelings would raise questions.

In summary, it was assumed that by getting information about, and/or descriptions of, various activities, traits, symptoms, etc., it would then be possible to make inferences or generalizations about developmental progression within a certain aspect of development; and from these inferences and generalizations, an assessment of overall progression *and* of pathology could be made.

Social Development (Object Relations)

The people to whom a child characteristically relates,

and the ways in which he relates to them, can give some indication of his progression in development. It would be expected that he would have an ever-expanding number of relationships as he matures, with differentiation in the quality of the relationships, along with increasing interest in and sensitivity to the needs and reactions of others.

Expanding Social Relations

The number of people with whom a child has relationships increases with age, and the nature of these relationships changes with development. Development moves from no discrimination of individuals to a relationship only with the mothering person, to relationships with other family members, then with peers, and ultimately with socializing agencies in the community. Though in the beginning, members of the family (especially the mother) are of greatest significance, from about age three on, playmates becoms increasingly important. Thus, it is possible to look at the extent to which a child is able to relate to other people within and outside the family and to assess his social developmental status. Inferences can be made as to how exclusive the child's relationship is to his mother and to other family members, and as to what capacity he has to relate to peers.

Separation

With age, there is also expected the development of the capacity to separate from mother and/or the family, in space and time. This is related to the expansion of the child's social interest. Indices of the child's capacity to separate would include such items as the feelings aroused in him by the act of being separated from his mother and/or by her absence for a period of time; the ability to visit relatives and peers for a short time and/or for overnight; the ability to attend nursery school regularly; and the ability to attend day camp. Intense separation anxiety would raise questions about the child's developmental progression in this area and would be taken as a symptom.

Quality of Relationships

The quality of a child's social relationships also changes as he matures — from using the "other" only as an instrument for the satisfaction of his own needs to mutually satisfying, intimate, long-lasting friendships. Therefore, the type and intensity of his relationships with others give some indication of the child's current level of social development. For example, a child may be able to have only superficial, transient relationships; or he may be able to relate only in a clinging, overdependent way.

It is possible to look at the dominant features of the child's relationships with others, including the kind of wishes the child has in a relationship, the needs that are satisfied, and the concerns present in the relationship. In his relating to others, the child shows behaviors that reflect his concerns associated with each phase of development. Based on psychoanalytic developmental psychology, it is expected that each child would pass through several stages during his preschool and kindergarten years (see Chapter 5 on "phase development"). Thus, it is possible to assess some aspects of the social relationships by looking at the needs satisfied in the relationship (such as needs for contact, attention, approval, help, admiration), the expectations and wishes, and the techniques used in the relationship (such as demanding, whining, bossing, seducing).

At the earilest age, the "other" exists only for the child's satisfaction and is expected to know and to meet his wishes and needs. The child experiences the mother or mother surrogate as indispensable for need gratification (food, play, help) and for comfort. Clinging serves the purpose of immediacy of gratification and protection. The young child often shows a need for excessive body contact, with tendencies to "melt" with the other. He needs mother's presence and support, and tries to please her and get her approval. Relationships are characterized by passivity, lack of initiative, excessive reliance on the "other" (for dressing, toileting, and other tasks). Helplessness is an expression of the lack of independence, an invitation for mother to do things for the child. As a child becomes aware of himself as separate from others, he tries to control them and/or tries not to be controlled by them. There may be conflict with them and angry interaction; the child may appear negativistic, dominating, or bossy in his relationships. Following this, relationships may be competitive; the child may appear exhibitionistic, attention-seeking, challenging, rivalrous; and at a later phase the child may characteristically be manipulative, coy, and flirtatious in his relationships.

Concern for Others

It is also possible to look for evidences of the child's interest in and sensitivity to the needs and reactions of others. As he becomes older, he would be expected to show concern for the well-being of the "other," to show empathy. There would also be expected an increasing capacity to adapt to the needs of others, to share with them. Along with this kind of consideration, there may be indications of a developing sensitivity to others' moods and momentary feelings.

Impact on Others

In addition to the above, we can look at the child's developing impact on his social environment — the responses of others to him. Who responds to him? And in what ways do they respond? We can look at him in one-to-one relationships and look at him in his participation as a member of a group, to see his effect on others and on their activities.

Developmental Assessment Outline

Social development is an aspect of development that is easily observable, particularly in the way the child relates to his classmates and teachers, as well as in the way he relates to his parents, other family members, and other adults in the environment. Many teachers spontaneously comment on the child's relationships in writing their progress reports on children. To ask that this aspect of development be included in a short assessment outline, therefore, does not make the unreasonable demand that teachers or day-care workers become clinicians. Yet this type of information is significant in assessing the child's developmental progression.

Items for a short assessment outline were extracted from what had been included in the intensive, comprehensive study of the nonclinical children. It was found that by taking these particular items together, there could result a valid and reliable gross indication of the child's social developmental status.[2]

Emotional Development (Affect)

Every action of a child occurs within the context of a feeling-tone, and often the feeling-tone is more important than what the child is thinking. The kinds of feelings the child has, and the way in which he handles them, may indicate whether he is developing according to expectations. At the same time, emotional factors can interfere with developmental progression in other areas, or with various aspects of functioning. For example, the feelings of a child may affect his learning — or lack of learning.

Characteristic Mood

Although not a developmental variable, it is important to assess the characteristic mood of a child because of the impact this may have on other aspects of development. By "characteristic mood" is meant that mood which is most typical of the child, that mood which the child seems to experience more than any other mood. Is this a child who is

---

[2]See Appendix B for discussion of validity and reliability.

usually happy-contented-satisfied or a child who is usually anxious-fearful-apprehensive or a child who is usually angry-annoyed-irritated or a child who is usually sad-depressed-unhappy-disappointed?

In assessing the child, it is significant whether he conveys a feeling of hope and confidence; or a feeling of despair, hopelessness, and discouragement; or a feeling of constant anxiety. Any child may show transient episodes of anxiety or fear, and he then acts in a way to get over this anxiety. But it is not expected that anxiety would usually be a child's characteristic affect.

In general, teachers are aware of the characteristic emotional tone of a child — which children are usually content and satisfied, and which are usually discontent or dissatisfied; which are frequently angry and which are frequently sad.

Variety and Range of Feelings

With age, it is expected that children develop and show an increasing differentiation in the variety and range of feelings. They become increasingly verbal about their feelings and recognize more and more different feelings. Instead of just talking about feeling "good" or not good," they can talk about feeling "glad" or "sad."

Emotional Expression

Children also show an increase in the stability of their emotions and a decrease in the intensity of expression. The child moves from uncontrolled, immediate, motor (global) expression to more controlled, delayed, and verbal expression. Children learn the conscious use of culturally approved gestures, facial expressions, and statements. With age, there is a decrease in the random discharge of emotion and an increase in the purposive "directing" of expression. The more diffuse, uninhibited expressions, such as screaming or agitated movements, are replaced by verbal techniques, such as describing and explaining.

There is increasing mastery of "the chaotic state within," so that there can be a certain amount of expressive freedom at the same time that the child is learning to meet cultural expectations of what is appropriate and what is inappropriate in the expression of his feelings in response to specific precipitating conditions or to ongoing situations; and where it is appropriate to express the feelings and where inappropriate.

There is a development from the immediate expression of feelings, the sudden outbursts, to delayed expression. Feelings come "under control." At the earliest ages, affect is likely to be quite labile, with sudden changes and frequent tantrums. But during the nursery school and kindergarten years, it is expected that emotional life will become more stable.

Social Orientation

There is an increasingly social orientation in the expression of feelings. The child moves from being completely self-centered (insensitive to others) to becoming more sensitive to others' feelings and responses, and to experiencing feelings such as compassion, sympathy, tenderness, guilt, embarrassment.

Developmental Assessment Outline

The emotional aspect is an area of development that is often mentioned spontaneously by teachers in their reports; and therefore can be assessed in a more systematic way by them without involving a great deal of training or a shift in the teachers' accustomed ways of looking at children. Again, the emphasis is on overall judgments rather than on counting specific behaviors.

As with social development, it is possible to use as indices of emotional development overt aspects of behavior observable to teachers and child care workers. The items to be included in the short assessment outline were selected from the material that had been used in the intensive clinical study of the population of nonclinical children. The various statistical analyses had shown that, taken together, the items offered a valid and reliable gross indication of the child's emotional developmental status.[3]

---

[3]See Appendix B for discussion of validity and reliability.

Criteria for Assessing
SOCIAL DEVELOPMENT

Phase	Characteristic, expected, typical	Relationship with Mother Uncharacteristic, unexpected, untypical, pathological	
		Ranging from:	To:
1. Infant: birth to 1½ (Oral Phase)	Need-fulfilling relationship, based on child's needs. Mother exists only for child's satisfaction, may be seen only as instrument to provide for satisfaction of needs. Child "wants" to be given everything and depends on mother for gratification. May see mother as powerful object to influence in order to get what is needed; may make efforts to please or win her. Fears loss of mother. Trusts mother to fulfill needs.	Predominantly a clinging relationship in which there is continual seeking to get needs satisfied. Wants to be given everything and does not make efforts to become independent. Constantly needs mother's presence, support, assurance; continually seeks contact; tries to win mother, please her, get her approval, sympathy. Appears overdependent, passive, obedient, overcompliant. Great urgency and intensity in relationship. Often insecure, apprehensive, tense, anxious in relating to mother.	Feels he cannot get what he wants from mother or get his needs satisfied and has given up trying. Lack of trust. Has turned away from mother, uninvolved with her, aloof, apathetic toward her. May avoid contact with mother, rebuff her, refuse her help. May appear precociously independent or may have turned to another adult as mother-substitute. Difficult for mother to satisfy; usually wants more than mother can give. Demanding, insistent, complaining, impatient in relation to mother. Greedy, insatiable; acts as if there is a feeling of deprivation.
2. Toddler: 1½ to 3 (Anal Phase)	Strong relationship with negativistic tinge. Control an important factor. Attempts to control and at times may torment, harass, tease. Much ambivalence, sometimes with love predominating, sometimes with hate. Fears loss of mother's love. Negativism with insistence that mother be around (object is there and needed, though child says No).	Extremely controlling with mother. Dominating and bossy in relating to mother. Constantly ordering her about, telling her what to do. Extremely sensitive to mother's criticism. Cries easily. Feelings easily hurt by mother.	Extremely negativistic and defiant in relating to mother. Much strain in the relationship. "Difficult." Interaction intense, urgent, with much ambivalence. Child quarrelsome stubborn, obstinate. May torment or harass mother. Much angry interaction and conflict. Frequent arguing, fault-finding, scolding, interrupting, provoking, teasing.

Phase	Characteristic, expected, typical	Uncharacteristic, unexpected, untypical, pathological Ranging from:	To:
			Masochistic — provoking retaliation, hurting by mother; sadistic — cruel. May be destructive (I hate you and don't love you).
3. Differentiating Stage: 3 to 4½ (Phallic Phase)	Developing awareness of his/her own sexual identity; may affect some interaction with mother. Continued bids for mother's attention, admiration, and praise. Tries to show mother how big, attractive, powerful he/she is. Responsive to mother; more or less cooperative. Relationship mutually satisfying.	Overly concerned about sexual identity; uses it in exaggerated attempts to get mother's attention, admiration, and praise. Constantly showing mother how big, attractive and powerful he/she is — to get reassurance, approval. Overly responsive, cooperative.	Indifferent to sexual identity; denies any interest in mother; actively avoids her. Avoids attention and/or praise from mother; may even reject mother's attentions. Emphasizes smallness, powerlessness. Unresponsive, uncooperative.
4. Family Integration: Boy 4½ to 6 (Oedipal Phase)	With increasing awareness of his own sexual identity, more seductive with mother and more possessive of her. May identify with father and act protective with mother. Copies father's behavior toward mother. May show some concern about whether mother prefers father or him. Shows preference for mother rather than father. May play parents against each other. Objects to parents going out together. Friendly to mother; easily accepts her authority; turns	Extremely possessive with mother — rivalrous with father or siblings for mother; jealous of contacts mother has with others. Extremely seductive with mother, almost in caricatured, exaggerated ways. *Has* to show mother he is better than father and that father is no good. Adores and idealizes mother. Exaggerates masculine behavior, in relating to mother. Excessive interest in and sensitivity to mother's feelings, moods. Extreme concern for mother's well-being.	Consciously inhibits all contact with mother. Fearful of winning mother in competition with father. Fearful of retaliation by father if wins mother; avoids mother because of the danger. Great concern to show he is *not* a man, cannot win mother, is different from father. Inhibits masculine behavior in relating to mother. Lack of interest in or sensitivity to mother's feelings, moods. Lack of concern for mother's well-being.

Phase	Characteristic, expected, typical	Uncharacteristic, unexpected, untypical, pathological	
		Ranging from:	To:
	to her when necessary for help. Shows some interest in and sensitivity to mother's feelings, moods. Shows some concern for mother's well-being.		
5. Family Integration: Girl 4½ to 6 (Oedipal Phase)	With increasing awareness of her own sexual identity, more competitive with mother for father. May show some hostility toward mother; but also fear of retaliation and fear of hurting mother (who is also a love object). May anticipate being harmed by mother. Tries to be like mother, identify with her but to show her up; or may inhibit feminine behavior and appear tomboyish. May show some anxiety about being separated from mother because of own wishful fantasies. Objects to parents going out together. May play parents against each other. Shows some interest in and sensitivity to mother's feelings, moods. Shows some concern for mother's well-being.	Great concern to show father prefers her to mother, that she is "better" than mother. "Puts down" mother. Exaggerates own femininity. Extremely rivalrous with mother. Shows much hostility to mother. Lacks any concern about mother's well-being. **Lacks any interest in or sensitivity to mother's feelings, moods.** Avoids mother.	Fearful about competing with mother; fearful of retaliation by mother, so actively avoids contact with father. Shows preference for mother rather than father. Great concern to show she is *not a woman*, cannot win father, is different from mother. Inhibits *all* feminine behavior. Intense anxiety about separation because of own fantasies. Excessive interest in and sensitivity to mother's feelings, moods. Extreme concern for mother's well-being.

Criteria for Assessing
SOCIAL DEVELOPMENT

Phase	Characteristic, expected, typical	Separation	
		Uncharacteristic, unexpected, untypical, pathological	
		Ranging from:	To:
1. Infant: birth to 1½ (Oral Phase)	No clear differentiation of self. Sense of identity undeveloped and fluid — as if mother (or mother-substitute) should know his wishes-needs and meet them. Mother exists only for child's satisfaction of needs. No existence of her own. Depends on mother for gratification; needs to be given everything. Mother's other concerns or activities are experienced as rejection-desertion. Beginning to notice "the world" — reach out for and handle what is seen; respond to surroundings — sounds, sights. Beginning to distinguish between self and world around him. Can accept brief separation from mother, after some protest. Some object constancy, so positive image of mother maintained. Beginning to develop ability to accept mother-substitutes (either other family members or familiar baby-sitters).	Sense of identity continues undeveloped and fluid; no clear differentiation of self even begins. Needs to be given everything and does not make efforts to satisfy own needs. Little interest in "the world"; little or no attempt to reach out for anything; seldom manipulates things; "shuts out" the world.	Cannot tolerate separation. Exclusive in relating to mother; able to have relationship *only* with mother. Great anxiety when mother is not present. *Or*, has turned away from mother. Feels he cannot get needs satisfied by her or get what he wants. May appear unresponsive to her. May avoid contact with mother, rebuff her. No difficulty separating from mother. Has abandoned her, rejected her ("I don't want you because you don't satisfy my needs, don't give me love.")

Phase	Characteristic, expected, typical	Uncharacteristic, unexpected, untypical, pathological	
		Ranging from:	To:
2. Toddler: 1½ to 3 (Anal Phase)	Aware of self as separate from others — trying to control others and/or trying not to be controlled by others. Aware of some of own wants, likes and dislikes. May talk about self as a third person ("Betty wants that.") Looks at and describes self from viewpoint of (significant) others — e.g., "good boy." Able to leave mother and play by self in another room; can tolerate some distance from mother. Temporary separations from mother can be lengthened. Can move out toward other family members and familiar adults. Temporary separations from mother and home are possible, to go with familiar adult, such as grandparent.	Extreme concern about maintaining separateness — not being controlled by others. Avoids mother and/or other family members. Physically distant as much of the time as possible. Prefers to visit grandparents, neighbors; be with strangers.	Fear of being separate — tries to be "one" with more powerful being — desperately clings. Loses self in desire to be "good," not lose love and acceptance of mother and/or other family members. More aware of approval-disapproval of mother and family than of own wants-likes.
3. Differentiating Stage: 3 to 4½ (Phallic Phase)	Aware of own sexual identity. Enjoys mother's presence but can accept being separated from rest of family and from home. After short transition period, can accept attending nursery school. Can exchange visits at homes of peers.	Individuation only in terms of sex; exaggeration of sexual identification; confusion re sexual identification; denial of sexual identification. Uses separation from mother-family-home to deny fears, weaknesses, vulnerability; prove strength, power, "bigness," courage. Too easily leaves mother at nursery school.	Uses inability to separate from mother-family-home to deny "growing up," power, strength; emphasizes smallness, helplessness. Unable to accept nursery school — unless mother stays with him all the time. Unable to visit peers.

Phase	Characteristic, expected, typical	Uncharacteristic, unexpected, untypical, pathological	
		Ranging from:	To:
4. Family Integration: 4½ to 6 (Oedipal Phase)	Aware of identification with and competition with same-sex parent; aware of identification with family — as a member of the family. Able to attend school regularly; able to accept overnight visits to homes of friends. Becoming aware of self as a member of the community. Identification with peers at school. Able to attend day-camp; be away from home for a weekend.	Overidentifies with same-sex parent; overidentifies with family. Not aware of other facets of individuation. Avoids mother or father because of danger from rivalry. Avoids family — away from home most of the time.	Intense anxiety about separation because of own fantasies. Has to stay near mother-family-home because of what might happen while he is gone. Unable to attend school regularly; unable to stay away from home overnight.

Criteria for Assessing
SOCIAL DEVELOPMENT

Relationship with Father

Phase	Characteristic, expected, typical	Uncharacteristic, unexpected, untypical, pathological	
		Ranging from:	To:
1. Infant: birth to 1½ (Oral Phase)	Recognition of father; some contact with father, and responsive to overtures from father, though prefers mother as caretaking person.	No relationship with father; unaware of father; unresponsive to father; uninvolved with him at all. Rejects father, pushes him away.	Clings to father, continually seeking contact with father. Relates to father as mother-substitute, to depend on and get his needs satisfied, give him affection. Prefers father to mother as caretaking person. Submissive, dependent, overcompliant with father. Continually tries to please father, get his approval and/or sympathy. Demanding of father; difficult to satisfy.
2. Toddler: 1½ to 3 (Anal Phase)	Relationship with father predominantly friendly. Enjoys being with father, but can accept being separated from him. Some **struggle re control; may try to boss, tell father what to do and how; may argue, defy.**	Minimal contact with father. Fearful of father, apprehensive, cautious, timid; shy. Anticipates father will not like him or accept him, and avoids father. Relationship with father appears transitory, shallow, superficial.	Unfriendly, extremely negativistic. Relationship intense, urgent, with much strain and anxiety. Child characteristically has angry interaction or conflict with father. Frequent arguing, finding fault, scolding, provoking, teasing. Extremely defiant, difficult, quarrelsome, hostile, stubborn, obstinate in relating to father. Masochistic — provoking retaliation, getting hurt by father; sadistic — cruel.

Phase	Characteristic, expected, typical	Uncharacteristic, unexpected, untypical, pathological	
		Ranging from:	To:
3. Differentiating Stage: 3 to 4½ (Phallic Phase)	Developing awareness of his/her own sexual identity may affect interaction with father. Continued bids for father's attention, admiration, and praise. Tries to show father how big, attractive, powerful he/she is. Boy may anticipate being harmed (castrated) by father. Responsive to father; more or less cooperative with father. Relationship mutually satisfying.	Uses sexual identity in exaggerated attempts to get father's attention, admiration, and praise. Constantly showing father how big, attractive and powerful he/she is — to get reassurance, approval. Overly responsive to father; overly cooperative.	Indifferent to sexual identity; denies any interest in father; actively avoids him. Avoids attention and/or praise from father; may even reject father's attentions. Emphasizes smallness, powerlessness. Unresponsive, uncooperative with father.
4. Family Integration: Boy 4½ to 6 (Oedipal Phase)	With increasing awareness of his own sexual identity, more competitive with father for mother. May show some hostility toward father, but also fear of retaliation and fear of hurting father (who is also a love object). Tries to be like father, identify with him but to show him up; or may inhibit masculine behavior. May show some anxiety about being separated from father because of own wishful fantasies. Objects to parents going out together. May play parents against each other. Shows some interest in and sensitivity to father's feelings, moods. Shows some	Great concern to show mother prefers him to father, that he is "better" than father. "Puts down" father. Exaggerates own masculinity. Extremely rivalrous with father. Shows much hostility to father. Lacks any concern about father's well-being. Lacks any interest in or sensitivity to father's feelings, moods. Avoids father.	Fearful of competing with father; fearful of retaliation by father; so actively avoids contact with mother. Shows preference for father rather than mother. Great concern to show he is *not* a man, cannot win mother, is different from father. Inhibits *all* masculine behavior. Intense anxiety about separation because of own fantasies. Excessive interest in and sensitivity to father's feelings, moods. Extreme concern for father's well-being.

Phase	Characteristic, expected, typical	Uncharacteristic, unexpected, untypical, pathological	
		Ranging from:	To:
	concern for father's well-being. Shows preference for mother rather than father.		
5. Family Integration: Girl 4½ to 6 (Oedipal Phase)	With increasing awareness of her own sexual identity, more seductive with father and more possessive of him. May identify with mother and act solicitous with father. Copies mother's behavior toward father. May show some concern about whether father prefers mother or her. Shows preference for father rather than mother. May play parents against each other. Objects to parents going out together. Friendly to father; easily accepts his authority; turns to him when necessary for help. Shows some interest in and sensitivity to father's feelings, moods. Shows some concern for father's well-being.	Extremely possessive with father — rivalrous with mother or siblings for father; jealous of contacts father has with others. Extremely seductive with father, almost in caricatured, exaggerated ways. *Has* to show father she is better than mother and that mother is no good. Adores and idealizes father. Exaggerates feminine behavior in relating to father. Excessive interest in and sensitivity to father's feelings, moods. Extreme concern for father's well-being.	Consciously inhibits all contact with father. Fearful of winning father in competition with mother. Fearful of retaliation by mother if wins father; avoids father because of the danger. Great concern to show she is *not* a woman, cannot win father, is different from mother. Inhibits feminine behavior in relation to father. Lack of interest in or sensitivity to father's feelings, moods. Lack of concern for father's well-being.

Criteria for Assessing
SOCIAL DEVELOPMENT

Relationship with Siblings

Phase	Characteristic, expected, typical	Uncharacteristic, unexpected, untypical, pathological	
		Ranging from:	To:
1. Infant: birth to 1½ (Oral Phase)	Recognition of siblings; some contact with them, responsive to overtures from siblings; some interest in their activities. At times tries to imitate, copy, sibling behaviors.	No relationship with siblings; unaware of them; unresponsive to them; uninvolved with them in any way; no interest in their activities. Rejects siblings, pushes them away.	Relates to siblings as mother-substitute, to depend on and get needs satisfied; prefers sibling to mother as caretaking person. Always plays "baby" with sibling. Submissive, dependent, overcompliant. Continually tries to please siblings, get their approval and/or sympathy. Clinging with siblings. Demanding of siblings; difficult to satisfy.
2. Toddler: 1½ to 3 (Anal Phase)	Enjoys being with siblings, but can accept being separated from them. Some struggle re control; may try to boss them, tell them what to do and how; may try to control by "mothering." May argue, provoke, tease, at times.	Fearful of siblings, apprehensive, cautious, timid, shy. Avoids contact with siblings. Anticipates siblings will not like him and/or accept him. Relationship with siblings appears transitory, shallow, superficial.	Usually in conflict with siblings. Unfriendly, extremely negativistic. Relationship intense, urgent, with much strain and anxiety. Angry interaction, frequent arguing, finding fault, scolding, provoking, teasing. Extremely defiant, difficult, quarrelsome, hostile, stubborn, obstinate.

Phase	Characteristic, expected, typical	Uncharacteristic, unexpected, untypical, pathological	
		Ranging from:	To:
3. Differentiating Stage: 3 to 4½ (Phallic Phase)	Can participate in some play with siblings, can take turns and share. Asserts self with siblings, but shows some sensitivity to needs and feelings of siblings. Competes with siblings for attention and for toys. Feels "close" to same-sex sibling. May engage in sex play with sibling.	Inhibits self-assertion with siblings. Overly concerned about taking turns, sharing. Inhibits competition with siblings. "Too nice" with siblings; "too generous." Extremely sensitive to needs and feelings of siblings.	Extremely competitive with siblings, in all areas. Extremely assertive with siblings. No sensitivity to needs and feelings of siblings.
4. Family Integration: 4½ to 6 (Oedipal Phase)	Reciprocal relations with siblings. "Family" play with siblings. Can lead or follow. Easily shares, takes turns. Friendly, responsive, cooperative with siblings, most of the time. Shows interest in and sensitivity to siblings' moods. Shows concern for siblings' well-being.	Relates as if much younger child, using techniques of earlier phases. No interest in or sensitivity to siblings' feelings, moods. No concern for siblings' well-being.	Excessive interest in and sensitivity to siblings' feelings, moods. Extreme concern for siblings' well-being.

Criteria for Assessing
SOCIAL DEVELOPMENT

Relationship with Teacher

Phase	Characteristic, expected, typical	Uncharacteristic, unexpected, untypical, pathological	
		Ranging from:	To:
1. Infant: birth to 1½ (Oral Phase)	Relates to teacher as a mother-substitute, to depend on and get his needs satisfied, to give him care and affection.	Completely unresponsive to teacher; uninvolved with teacher. Apathetic, withdrawn. Distant in relating to teacher.	Overdependent on teacher; excessively clinging; constantly trying to get contact, sympathy, attention. Does not individualize teachers. Overly demanding, insistent, impatient in relating to teacher. Difficult to satisfy; usually wants more than teacher can give; complaining.
2. Toddler: 1½ to 3 (Anal Phase)	Struggle for control with teacher. Tries to tell her what to do and how to do it. At times, bossy; at times may argue, defy, be negativistic.	Fearful of teacher, apprehensive, cautious, timid, shy. Anticipates teacher will not like him or accept him and actively avoids teacher. Relationship may appear transitory, shallow, superficial.	Unfriendly to teacher; extremely negativistic, defiant. Quarrelsome with teacher; hostile, stubborn, obstinate. "Difficult" child. Much angry interaction and conflict with teacher; arguing, finding fault, scolding, provoking, teasing.
3. Differentiating Stage: 3 to 4½ (Phallic Phase)	At times may try to identify with teacher and be like her; at other times may compete with teacher. Bids for teacher's attention, admiration, praise. Able to assert own desires and ideas to teacher. Able to ask for help.	Extremely competitive with teacher. Overidentifies with teacher. Constantly seeking teacher's attention — e.g., by clowning, "acting up," "being difficult," "showing off," making excessive demands. Extremely assertive with teacher.	Ignores teacher. Avoids teacher's attention. Unable to assert himself with teacher, unable to make desires and needs known.

Phase	Characteristic, expected, typical	Uncharacteristic, unexpected, untypical, pathological	
		Ranging from:	To:
4. Family Integration: 4½ to 6 (Oedipal Phase)	Friendly in relating to teacher. Usually responsive, cooperative. Easily accepts teacher's authority and teacher's help. With awareness of his own sexual identity, boy may act "gallant," "charming," "seductive" with teacher. Girl may be coy. Shows some interest in and sensitivity to teacher's feelings, moods. Shows some concern for teacher's well-being.	Overly friendly with teacher; overly cooperative; "too nice." *Has* to accept teacher's authority and teacher's help. Excessive interest in and sensitivity to teacher's feelings, moods. Extreme concern for teacher's well-being.	Avoids teacher; makes active effort to stay at a distance from teacher. Unresponsive to teacher. Will not accept teacher's authority or teacher's help. No interest in or sensitivity to teacher's feelings, moods. No concern for teacher's well-being.

Criteria for Assessing
SOCIAL DEVELOPMENT

Relationship with Other Children

Phase	Characteristic, expected, typical	Uncharacteristic, unexpected, untypical, pathological	
		Ranging from:	To:
1. Infant: birth to 1½ (Oral Phase)	Notices other children. Some interest in other children for brief periods of time — as an observer. Some response to overtures to other children. Characteristically, spends most of the time playing with own hands and feet, materials, toys and/or equipment, household items. Other children show some interest in him; give some attention to him; make some overtures toward him.	Completely unresponsive to other children, uninterested in them, uninvolved with them. Unrelated to other children. Apathetic, withdrawn. Rejects other children; pushes them away. Most of the time in solitary play, physically and emotionally distant from other children — "isolated." May wander around alone, aimless, with no focus. Most of the time this child has no effect on other children. They are oblivious to him or not interested in him: They ignore him.	Relates to other children as mother-substitute to depend on and get needs satisfied. Always a "baby," always a "follower." Submissive, dependent, overcompliant, clinging, with other children. Continually tries to please, get their approval and/or sympathy. Demands more than other children are willing to give. Other children try to avoid him. Sees other children as treating him unfairly, picking on him. Complaining.
2. Toddler: 1½ to 3 (Anal Phase)	Some struggle with other children for control; tries to tell them what to do and how to do it. May try to take the "authority" role, or to control by "mothering." At times bossy, at times arguing. Most of the time in play parallel to other children. May play alone, but next to another child and may be doing same things as other child. Much of the time this child arouses interest of other children who may watch his activity.	Fearful, apprehensive, cautious, timid in relating to other children. Feels other children will not like him or accept him; avoids them. Shy. Lack of interaction; distant with other children. Avoids all fights or arguments. Any relationships with other children appear transitory, shallow, superficial. Very controlled, inhibited in play with other children. Cannot "let himself go."	Unfriendly in relating to other children. Defiant, negativistic, quarrelsome, hostile. Frequent angry interaction and conflict; frequent arguing, finding fault, scolding, interrupting, provoking, teasing. Bullies other children; makes them cry. Sadistic, cruel. Torturing possessiveness. Masochistic — provokes other children to hurt him. Easily offended by other children.

Phase	Characteristic, expected, typical	Uncharacteristic, unexpected, untypical, pathological	
		Ranging from:	To:
3. Differentiating Stage: 3 to 4½ (Phallic Phase)	Can participate in play with other children. Asserts self, but also shows some sensitivity to needs and feelings of other children. Competes with other children for attention and for toys. Spends most of his time with one child who is special friend, but may also spend time with other children, or some time alone. Shows some social skills. Exchanges visits with other children. Much of the time, he arouses interest of other children who may try to participate with him in ongoing activity. Some children seek him out as playmate.	Inhibits self-assertion with other children. Inhibits competitiveness with other children. Extremely sensitive to needs and feelings of other children. "Too generous," "too nice."	Extremely assertive with other children. Extremely competitive with other children. No sensitivity to needs and feelings of other children. Much of the time stimulates other children by his activity to point where they may act in an excited, uncontrolled way. Often has disruptive effect.
4. Family Integration: 4½ to 6 (Oedipal Phase)	Reciprocal relations with other children. Constancy and depth in relationships. Friendly, responsive, cooperative. Increasing social sensitivity, increasing social skills, sympathetic. Can lead or follow. Most of the time a participant in cooperative play with another child or a small group of children. Boys may prefer to play with other boys and girls with other girls. However, much more "family play" with girls and with boys.	Avoiding play with same-sex children; preferring to play with opposite sex children. *Has* to be leader.	Relates as if much younger child, using techniques of earlier phases. Can *only* be a follower.

Criteria for Assessing
SOCIAL DEVELOPMENT

Phase	Characteristic, expected, typical	Participation in Groups of Children Uncharacteristic, unexpected, untypical, pathological	
		Ranging from:	To:
1. Infant: birth to 1½ (Oral Phase)	May passively partipate just by being present in the same situation with other children.		
2. Toddler: 1½ to 3 (Anal Phase)	Sometimes interested in ongoing activities of a small group; occasionally can function in a group situation.	Avoids groups and/or not interested in groups. Minimal participation in groups. Cannot function as a member of a group and/or does not become involved in group activities. May be oblivious to group; or fearful and anxious.	*Has* to get into the group. Pushes himself into groups. Becomes overexcited and overstimulated by group and may act in uncontrolled way. Erratic in group participation.
3. Differentiating Stage: 3 to 4½ (Phallic Phase)	Much of the time can function adequately as a member of a group. Can participate actively, making contributions, offering ideas or suggestions. Alert and responsive in discussions. Active in some group projects.	Cannot function well in group — too assertive, too competitive; alienates other children in group. Unable to function cooperatively. Tries unsuccessfully to manipulate other group participants.	Passive observer in group. Unable to take initiative; unable to arouse the interest of other members of group.
4. Family Integration: 4½ to 6 (Oedipal Phase)	Most of the time he is in small group situations with two or three other children. Participates actively as group member, cooperates with others. Creative in group situation; invents new play. Can lead at times, follow at times.	*Has* to be a leader in the group. Tries to be "autocratic parent." Does not know how to charm others in group into accepting his ideas.	Sterotyped, unoriginal in group play. Copies other group members; cannot originate group activities. Can function in group as a follower. Denies interest in group and/or avoids group.

Criteria for Assessing
EMOTIONAL DEVELOPMENT

Variety and Intensity of Affect; Characteristic Mood

Phase	Characteristic, expected, typical	Uncharacteristic, unexpected, untypical, pathological	
		Ranging from:	To:
1. Infant: birth to 1½ (Oral Stage)	Periods of tension (pain)-irritability followed by periods of contentment (pleasure). Glow of contentment when satiated and needs met. Most of the time conveys sense of general comfort. Occasional indications of frustration-anger; anxiety. Beginning to show some feelings of trust, some affection.	Persistent, unrelieved tension (pain) — irritability, with subsequent anger (rage) and/or exhaustion. Most of the time irritable, cranky, fussy restless, discontented, uncomfortable. Frequent signs of frustration-anger.	Chronically depressed, dejected, or apathetic. Most of the time unresponsive, listless, air of hopelessness. Indifferent.
2. Toddler: 1½ to 3 (Anal Phase)	Child is able to experience and to express some variety of feelings. Much of the time, strong "peak" feelings; excited, lively kinds of feelings — enthusiasm, interest, joy. Unpleasant moods or sudden outbursts may occasionally occur, but are soon over.	Extreme intensities of feelings are experienced; high levels of tension. Shifts from extremes of "high" and "low." Great excitability. Rages. Much disgust. Strong reactions to control by others. Outbursts frequently occur and may last a long while, in attempts to control others. Characteristic mood is angry, attacking, annoyed, resentful.	Child is able to experience and to express only a limited variety of feelings. Child expresses primarily one or two feelings. Some feelings are *seldom* experienced or expressed; some feelings are "never" experienced or expressed (i.e., certain affect is repressed, inhibited, denied). Child may appear bland, sullen, solemn.

Phase	Characteristic, expected, typical	Uncharacteristic, unexpected, untypical, pathological	
		Ranging from:	To:
3. Differentiating Stage: 3 to 4½ (Phallic Phase)	Increasing differentiation in the variety of feelings experienced and expressed. Child is able to experience a moderate range of affect — more so with his own family than with other people. Somewhat subdued feelings; experience of affect is mild. Characteristic mood is satisfied, content, pleased, happy. Evidence of some feelings of embarrassment, shame, self-consciousness.	Extremely strong, intense emotions. Rage, fury. Characteristic mood is attacking, "hyper"-active.	Child is able to experience a small range of affect; little variety of affect. Child has little awareness of variation in feelings. Characteristic mood is anxious, apprehensive, fearful, insecure and/or joyless, unhappy, sad, disappointed. Affect is inhibited or restricted, so that child is unaware of variation in feelings.
4. Family Integration: 4½ to 6 (Oedipal Phase)	Great differentiation in the variety of feelings experienced and expressed. Expressions of tenderness, pity, sympathy, compassion beginning to appear; also guilt. Sensitive to others' feelings and responses.	Extreme feelings.	Extreme constriction of feelings. Lack of feelings for others.

Criteria for Assessing
EMOTIONAL DEVELOPMENT

Phase	Characteristic, expected, typical	Expression of Affect Uncharacteristic, unexpected, untypical, pathological	
		Ranging from:	To:
1. Infant: Birth to 1½ (Oral Phase)	Affect expressed immediately. Undifferentiated, global responses. Expression of feelings often with whole body. Also, smiling, crying, grimacing; making of sounds, agitated movements.	Cries easily. Violent displays of undirected energy. Screaming, kicking, holding breath, hitting head against wall or furniture, biting self.	Subdued expression of affect. Whimpering, moaning, whining, silent staring.
2. Toddler: 1½ to 3 (Anal Phase)	At times, short delay in expression. Expression of feelings is in actions more than in words — in body movements, gestures, smiling, crying. Occasionally child may say he feels "good" or "not good." Child is able to express some variations in feelings.	Uncontrolled in expressing affect. Unable to delay expression — affect is expressed immediately and with great intensity, e.g., screaming, throwing self on floor, agitated movements (temper tantrums), throwing things. Explosions of messy, destructive behavior; fury.	Feelings are expressed by brooding, sulking, whining. Outbursts rarely occur. Unpleasant moods may persist for long periods. Child primarily expresses one or two feelings.
3. Differentiating Stage: 3 to 4½ (Phallic Phase)	Some verbal expression of feelings, e.g., I'm mad, I'm happy. Also, conscious use of gestures, postures, facial expressions, body movements, to express feelings. Feelings expressed openly and directly (girls less open than boys in expressing feelings). A "settling down" for both sexes in expression of feelings.	Feelings may be expressed in an artificial, exaggerated way. Child "overdramatizes" expression of feelings, is histrionic as a way of getting attention, of exhibiting self, showing off. Affect is labile; rapid and sudden shifts. Expression of affect may seem inappropriate to the precipitating conditions or to the	Child expresses some affect, but there is restraint, guardedness, hesitation — within the family, as well as outside. Affect is inhibited or restricted. Feelings may be expressed indirectly or in devious ways, e.g., in fantasy. Unhappy moods may persist for unusually long periods of time. (More often seen with girls than with boys at

Phase	Characteristic, expected, typical	Uncharacteristic, unexpected, untypical, pathological	
		Ranging from:	To:
	Increasing mastery of the chaotic emotional states within; expression of affect can be delayed to some extent, is under better control. Expression of affect seems appropriate to the situation. Affect stable, though occasional outbursts occur. Displays of anger of short duration.	ongoing situation — either as an overreaction or as a "wrong" reaction. Affective expression is extreme and/or intense.	this age.) Face may appear impassive, frozen. Feelings "held in."
4. Family Integration: 4½ to 6 (Oedipal Phase)	Increasingly able to express feelings verbally rather than in actions. Increasingly able to express a range of feelings with peers and teachers, as well as with own family members. Increasingly able to delay expression. (Boys more often open or intense in expressing feelings than girls; boys more often open than at earlier age.) Girls cry more than boys.	Regression to earlier ways of expressing feelings, e.g., nonverbal.	Affective expression is overcontrolled. Child expresses only a very limited variety of feelings.

Chapter 4
Aspects of Development
— Ego Development

The "ego" refers to those functions which deal with the child's capacity to assess external and internal reality and to deal with it. This would include evaluating situations, as well as evaluating the individual's own strengths and weaknesses. The ego permits the individual to learn from his experiences and to achieve his goals. It coordinates the demands of his own inner drives with the demands and pressures of the external world. It decides whether, in terms of the external realities, it is reasonable for the individual to act on his fantasies.

The equipment an individual has for coping with the world includes his capacities as well as his abilities — his perception, motility, speech, intelligence. In his functioning within social situations, he uses this equipment to organize, synthesize, and integrate his experiences.

How the child functions in various enviroments and how he copes with frustrating situations, whether he is able to make decisions and the kinds of decisions he makes, in what ways he adapts to reality — in short, his mastery of himself and his world — are indications of the level and quality of the child's ego developmental progression.

Motor Development

During the preschool and kindergarten years, the

child's physical activity increases and becomes broader, smoother, and more strenuous. The child develops more control of his physical movements, which include both his gross coordination and his fine eye/hand coordination. He becomes more agile and more poised in motor achievement; and his fine motor activities show more dexterity and more precision.

He may show off his physical skills and achievements by stunts, tricks, or "special performance."

Speech

At the same time, he is acquiring more words and learning to use these words more effectively in communicating. He talks more, and his speech becomes more comprehensible, better articulated, and more complex grammatically. He can use language to express desires, describe events, exchange information, ask questions.

Communication moves in the direction from egocentric to sociocentric; from thinking out loud to himself and engaging in monologues, to directing his language toward others and trying to influence their actions and thoughts. Gradually, he learns to use language to plan activities with others and to coordinate group activities.

Mental Development

There is also development in the use of the individual's mental equipment — his intelligence, creativity, judgment, anticipation, planning, curiosity. He expands his capacity to perceive the world, explore it, and act within it. Behavior is increasingly organized and yet can be adaptable and spontaneous. He develops more creativity in the use of materials and/or equipment. He improves in making judgments and in decision-making.

The child moves from concrete to abstract thinking, from perception to conception to explanation to inference;[1] from magical thinking to realistic thinking. He becomes better able to differentiate between fantasy and reality. He develops space concepts such as near-far, on-under, next-to; time concepts such as now-later-before; number concepts such as larger-smaller, more-less.

The intelligence of the child is considered a very important ego function. It permits the teachers (and parent) to know how much cognitive stimulation the child might respond to. Also it permits judgment about the capacity of the child to learn from experiences and to apply this learning in new situations. And in the school setting or in other learning situations, it permits grouping the children more or less homogeneously when this is desired.

Development of Competence

During these early years, there is also the development of self-sufficiency and competence. The child shows increasing autonomy, independence, purposiveness. He becomes more responsible for himself. He learns to feed himself, toilet himself, and dress himself. There is an increased emphasis on mastering activities and on mastering the daily realities.

The child also becomes more capable of controlling his impulses, more capable of delaying gratification and accepting substitute gratification, more capable of tolerating frustration and better able to handle stresses, demands, and pressures. In difficult situations, he does not immediately "give up" or "go to pieces."

Along with this, the child develops his ability to tolerate moderate amounts of anxiety and develops ways of dealing with his own anxiety through various "defense mechanisms."

He shows progression in learning and may compete with peers in this area. His attention span is increasing, as is his interest in asking questions. He seems eager to learn. He becomes interested in intellectual functioning and learn-

[1]See Dorothy Flapan, *Children's Understanding of Social Interaction* (New York: Teachers College Press, Columbia University, 1968).

ing, and seems to get satisfaction and pleasure from intellectual achievements.

Social and Sexual Identity

The child shows a developing awareness of himself as a person, with a social and sexual identity. He comes to recognize himself as a member of his family and of his social group in the community, as well as recognizing his membership in a specific sexual group.

Developmental Assessment Outline

Ego development is the aspect that has been most emphasized in the past in assessing young children, because it is obvious and thus easily available to teachers, day-care workers, and public health specialists. Motor functioning and intellectual functioning are behaviors typically observed in a school situation. This aspect is already quite familiar to teachers; in fact, it has often been used by them in their own evaluations of children. Because of their previous experience with this aspect, it is the easiest for teachers to make judgments about. In addition, teachers are in a good position to make such judgments without the need for special psychological tests.

The items chosen for the short assessment outline are only a small proportion of what had been assessed in the comprehensive, clinical study of the nonclinical sample of children attending community nursery schools. However, experience showed that together these items could be taken as a valid and reliable gross indication of the child's ego developmental status.[2]

---

[2]See Appendix B for discussion of validity and reliability.

Criteria for Assessing
EGO DEVELOPMENT

Phase	Characteristic, expected, typical	Mastery Uncharacteristic, unexpected, untypical, pathological	
		Ranging from:	To:
1. Infant: birth to 1½ (Oral Phase)	In the beginning, complete dependence for physical needs and bodily care. Bodily needs dependent on outside — to be turned, moved, fed, dressed, toileted. Beginnings of mastery — turning, sitting, crawling, walking, feeding self, reaching for objects. Needs much help. Signals hunger and discomfort and desire for assistance. Beginning to distinguish between self and world around him. Handling toys, pots, stuffed animals, etc. Pushing and/or pulling toys.	More attacking than dependent (fighting against object). Strenuous efforts to become independent. Cannot accept dependency.	Delay in turning, sitting, crawling, walking. Little or no attempts to reach for objects, feed self. Extreme helplessness. Gets help by crying, appearing helpless. Great dependency.
2. Toddler: 1½ to 3 (Anal Phase)	Gaining control of own body — feeds self, toilets self, tries to dress self. Asserting own controls (negative phase of independency). Does what *he* wants and in *his* way. Body movements coming under control, becoming smooth. Coordination good; dexterity good. Running, climbing. Good use of materials and equipment. Uses moderate variety of them, enjoys them, is discriminating in	Strong insistence on doing *everything* himself. Cannot let self depend on others. Fear of being controlled by others if depends on them. Overcontrol of body movements; body movements hesitant, overcautious. Restricted in physical activities. Sits unusually long time. Perseveration and/or repetition of tasks. Limited in use of materials and/or equipment.	Little or no attempts to control own body — feed self, toilet self, dress self. Does not accept controls. Little control of body movements, movements awkward, clumsy. Stumbles, falls, is sluggish. Coordination poor; dexterity poor. Constantly active, cannot "sit still." Poor use of materials and/or equipment. Sloppy and/or destructive with toys. Uses them in inappropriate, careless,

Phase	Characteristic, expected, typical	Uncharacteristic, unexpected, untypical, pathological	
		Ranging from:	To:
	their use. Attention span adequate in both self-originated and adult initiated projects. Can become engrossed in what he is doing. Can give many activities attention.	Avoids certain ones while dealing exclusively with others. Little imagination, creativity, flexibility, freedom in their use. Overly concerned about being careful in their use. Extremely prolonged attention span.	wasteful ways. No pleasure from "doing." Not easily involved. Distractible. Attention span short. Flies from one activity to another.
3. Differentiating Stage: 3 to 4½ (Phallic Phase)	Increasingly self-sufficient; needs little attention; most activities self-initiated; needs little help. Usually does not need to ask for help, but can ask for it when it is needed and/or after own efforts have not succeeded; can accept help. Asks for what he wants. Able to plan what he is going to do and carry out his plans. Usually "keeps trying," finishes what he begins. Functioning seems adequate for his age. Behavior organized, purposeful, yet adaptable and spontaneous. Girls more likely than boys to show inhibited mobility; more likely than boys to have good coordination, good dexterity.	*Cannot* ask for anything, because *has* to prove his strength and power to overcome his own doubts. Never asks for and usually rejects help, if help is offered. Will not accept help even when it is needed. *Cannot* ask for what he wants — sees it as admission of weakness. Techniques of getting what he wants appear to be stereotyped, nonadaptable, unspontaneous.	Unable to carry out what he wants to do. Few techniques for getting what he wants. Becomes easily discouraged about achieving what he set out to do and quickly asks for help or just "gives up" without finishing what he started. Behavior often appears to be disorganized, purposeless and/or nonadapting. Functioning seems inept, inadequate for age. Usually afraid to "try." Needs to have much structure and firmness from adult.

Phase	Characteristic, expected, typical	Uncharacteristic, unexpected, untypical, pathological	
		Ranging from:	To:
4. Family Integration: 4½ to 6 (Oedipal Phase)	Usually makes active attempt to master or cope with difficult, new, or challenging situation and usually is able to cope with it. Usually has a sense of his own power; aware of his abilities and uses them freely. Often takes initiative, takes responsibility, thinks for himself, tries to solve problems. Increasingly able to handle pressure from external environment. Good adaptation to school. Willing to take some risks; has courage. Appears moderately independent, autonomous, adaptable, flexible. Mastery of materials. Girls more likely than boys to show rigidity in functioning.	*Has* to deal with situation himself. Extreme determination. Forces himself to cope with it. *Has* to take responsibility. Rebuffs encouragement, reassurance, support from others. Insists on coping with difficult, new, or challenging situations himself. Even where unsuccessful in handling them himself, will not ask for help and will reject offers of help. Cannot acknowledge any shortcomings. Takes too many risks, constantly proving he has courage. Inflexible.	In difficult, new, or challenging situation, usually moves away and/or becomes passive. Usually does not try to master situation or else tries and is unable to cope with it. No sense of power. Feels helpless. Needs encouragement, reassurance, support from others to use his abilities. Seldom takes initiative; avoids or refuses responsibility. Cannot handle pressures from environment. Poor adaptation to school. Gives up easily, asks for help; discouraged. Afraid to try new things; afraid to risk.

Criteria for Assessing
EGO DEVELOPMENT

Phase	Characteristic, expected, typical	Communication Uncharacteristic, unexpected, untypical, pathological	
		Ranging from:	To:
1. Infant: birth to 1½ (Oral Phase)	Communicates by crying, by noises, by body movements, by gestures; smiles. Beginning to use simple words.	Incessant efforts to communicate, often frantic — crying, screaming, agitated body movements or gestures.	Little effort to communicate, even by cries and sounds. "Quiet baby"; "You hardly know the baby is there." Delay in attempts to use words.
2. Toddler: 1½ to 3 (Anal Phase)	Communicates by actions, one-word sentences, simple sentences. Language used to get needs met, to tell others what to do. Monologues.	Continuous talking — used as a way to control other people, to hold on to them. *Has* to comment on everything he is doing, everything he sees.	Inhibits communication. Little use of words. Can understand what is said and knows the words, but holds back. Maybe because negativistic, maybe because fearful.
3. Differentiating Stage: 3 to 4½ (Phallic Phase)	Able to express himself more or less adequately in speech. Adequate vocabulary. Able to exchange ideas, explain to others, ask questions, express desires, describe events, exchange information. Speaks with ease. Has good pronunciation.	Talks incessantly, cannot seem to restrain self. Talking may be to "show off," to compete with others, to get attention. Able to exchange ideas, explain to others, ask questions, but does these in extremely wordy way. Overwhelms others with a "flood of words" — even to the point where they may become confused.	Unable to express himself in speech. Inhibits communication; difficulty learning vocabulary. Little ability to exchange ideas, explain to others, ask questions. May be due to speech difficulty; may be because unable to assert self, unable to compete.

Phase	Characteristic, expected, typical	Uncharacteristic, unexpected, untypical, pathological	
		Ranging from:	To:
4. Family Integration: $4\frac{1}{2}$ to 6 (Oedipal Phase)	Communication moves from egocentric to sociocentric. Directs his language toward others and tries to influence their actions and thoughts. Learning to use language to plan activities with others and to coordinate group activities.	Communication resembles that of a younger child. Primarily egocentric. Absorbed in own words. Does not "communicate" in mutual give-and-take. Pushes others away with words.	Restricted communication. Minimally answers others. Does not initiate conversation. Limited vocabulary. Silent most of the time.

Criteria for Assessing
EGO DEVELOPMENT

Curiosity—Exploration, Thinking, Learning

Phase	Characteristic, expected, typical	Uncharacteristic, unexpected, untypical, pathological	
		Ranging from:	To:
1. Infant: birth to 1½ (Oral Phase)	Beginning to notice "the world," to show curiosity, to explore. Handles objects; crawls and pokes into corners, cupboards, shelves, etc. Alert; responsive to surroundings — to sight, sound, touch.	"Attacks" or "devours" the world with eyes, hands. *Has* to get into everything.	Little interest in "the world"; no explorations. Seldom manipulates things. Unresponsive to surroundings; sluggish quality. Limited awareness of things.
2. Toddler: 1½ to 3 (Anal Phase)	Curious about self and world. Expanding capacity to perceive world and explore it. Walks into various rooms, climbs, wanders in park; inquisitive. Shows interest and freedom to explore environment. Interest in solving problems. Thinking often unrealistic, magical.	"Pushes" to "find out" everything. Intense curiosity about everything. Much questioning. "Gets into" everything; frequently requires restraint by others.	Capacity to perceive world and explore it is inhibited. Shows little curiosity or freedom to explore. Inhibits curiosity about and interest in self and/or world. Any explorations are frightening, brief, erratic.
3. Differentiating Stage: 3 to 4½ (Phallic Phase)	Beginning to learn simple concepts of distance (space), time, number. Interest in learning. Some progress in learning — is about where he is expected to be for his chronological age. Expresses and shows curiosity about differences between boys and girls, about differences between children and	Great and intense interest in learning. Continual questioning, searching for answers. Great and intense curiosity about differences between boys and girls, about differences between children and adults. "Bound" by reality; does not permit himself to engage in fantasy.	Confusion about basic concepts of distance, time, number. Inhibits any interest in learning or in intellectual functioning. May be resistant to learning situations; may avoid learning situations. Little progress in learning — is behind what is expected for his chronological age.

Phase	Characteristic, expected, typical	Uncharacteristic, unexpected, untypical, pathological	
		Ranging from:	To:
	adults. Development from magical thinking to more realistic thinking. In contact with reality, though some fantasy. Able to maintain contact with reality and to interpret reality correctly. Better able than previously to differentiate between fantasy and reality.		Frequent and prolonged periods of time spent in fantasy. Difficulty interpreting reality; difficulty differentiating between fantasy and reality.
4. Family Integration: 4½ to 6 (Oedipal Phase)	Seems to realize his own potentialities in school and at home. Pleasure in intellectual functioning. Expansiveness; curiosity, freedom in exploring. Can anticipate, use judgment, plan, reason, organize, synthesize. Moving from concrete to abstract thinking; from perception to conception to explanation to inference and interpretation. Developing creativity in the use of materials and/or equipment. Improving in making judgments and in decision-making.	"Strains" to function beyond potentialities. Pushes self. "Overachiever." Little creativity in the use of materials and/or equipment.	Intellectual functioning does not seem to be up to child's potentialities. Learning difficulties; learning "blocks"; difficult to teach. "Underachiever." Poor in making judgments and/or in decision-making.

Criteria for Assessing
EGO DEVELOPMENT

Delay of Gratification; Frustration Tolerance; Impulse; Control

Phase	Characteristic, expected, typical	Uncharacteristic, unexpected, untypical, pathological	
		Ranging from:	To:
1. Infant: birth to 1½ (Oral Phase)	Unable to wait more than a short time; needs immediate gratification. Low frustration tolerance. Intense reaction when hungry, uncomfortable, not given what he wants, can't do what he is trying to do. Deprivation elicits aggressive response. Impulsive — grabs what he wants. Little or no control over impulses. Gradually develops some capacity for delay and some capacity to be diverted.	Cannot wait even a short time. No frustration tolerance. Any frustration or delay of gratification is intolerable, and he becomes frantic. No capacity for substitute gratification; no capacity to be diverted.	Waits and waits and waits. "Takes" delay and/or frustration without reacting as expected. Mild indication of hunger, discomfort, but then appears to resign himself.
2. Toddler: 1½ to 3 (Anal Phase)	Developing some control over impulses. As he feels assured satisfaction will follow, he shows capacity for increasing delay of gratification. Able to wait a moderate length of time for gratification. Also, increasing capacity for substitute gratification and increasing capacity to be diverted. Moderate frustration tolerance when he is not given what he wants or can't do what he is trying to do.	No expectation of getting what he wants. Immediate, intense reaction to any frustration or interference with desires.	Inhibition of impulses. Cannot permit self to act impulsively at any time. Appears to have extremely great frustration tolerance. Inhibits overt expressions of frustration. Gives impression of great patience.

Phase	Characteristic, expected, typical	Uncharacteristic, unexpected, untypical, pathological	
		Ranging from:	To:
	Increasing control over impulses, though still some impulsivity. Increasing capacity to delay gratification and/or accept substitute gratification — though he may express his disappointment and irritation. Increasingly able to tolerate frustration of not being given what he wants and of not being able to do what he is trying to do. Increasingly able to accept limitations of reality and postponement of gratification.		
3. Differentiating Stage: 3 to 4½ (Phallic Phase)	Able to tolerate moderate amounts of anxiety and has ways of dealing with anxiety through various "defense mechanisms."	Reacts as if still in oral or anal phase(see above).	Reacts as if still in oral or anal phase (see above).
4. Family Integration: 4½ to 6 (Oedipal Phase)	Shows moderate control over impulses. Can tolerate "average" delays of gratification, can accept substitute gratification at times. Able to tolerate moderate amounts of frustration as part of daily living.	Reacts as if still in oral or anal phase (see above).	Reacts as if still in oral or anal phase (see above).

Criteria for Assessing
EGO DEVELOPMENT

Social & Sexual Identification

Phase	Characteristic, expected, typical	Uncharacteristic, unexpected, untypical, pathological	
		Ranging from:	To:
1. Infant: birth to 1½ (Oral Phase)	No clear differentiation of self. Feels mother (or mother-substitute) should be able to "read his mind"; world should know his wishes. Sense of identity is poor and fluid. **Beginning to distinguish between self and world around him— respond to surroundings (sounds, sights); reach out for and handle what is seen.**		
2. Toddler: 1½ to 3 (Anal Phase)	Aware of self as separate from others — trying to control others and/or trying not to be controlled by others. May talk about self as a third person. Aware of some of own wants, likes and dislikes. Looks at and describes self from viewpoint of others, e.g., "good boy."		

Phase	Characteristic, expected, typical	Uncharacteristic, unexpected, untypical, pathological	
		Ranging from:	To:
3. Differentiating Stage: Boy 3 to 4½ (Phallic Phase)	Indications of identification of self as a boy — aware of sex-appropriate behaviors for a boy (e.g., more aggressive than girls in play and fantasy; more likely than girls to use overt conflict, with hitting, **shoving, wrestling; prefers activities and objects defined as appropriate for boys (e.g., guns).**	Exaggerated masculinity — almost caricature of stereotype of "boy." *Has* to reject any behaviors, interests, activities which might be considered "for girls."	Confusion re sexual identification; may identify with opposite sex; may slip from one sex to the other.
4. Differentiating Stage: Girl 3 to 4½ (Phallic Phase)	Indications of identification of self as a girl — aware of sex-appropriate behaviors for a girl (e.g., less aggressive than boys in play and fantasy; somewhat passive and dependent; more likely than boys to use verbal conflict rather than physical conflict); prefers activities and objects defined as appropriate for girls (e.g., cooking, jewelry).	Exaggerated feminity — almost caricatures stereotype of "girl." *Has* to reject any behaviors, interests, activities which might be considered "for boys."	Confusion re sexual identification; may identify with opposite sex; may slip from one sex to the other.
5. Family Integration: 4½ to 6 (Oedipal Phase)	Recognizes self as a member of his family and of his social group in the community. Boy identifies with and imitates father, e.g., in walk, mannerisms, voice, facial expressions, interests; girl identifies with and imitates mother.	Boy avoids father, wants to be different from father; imitates mother; doesn't like to play with other boys; doesn't like "masculine" activities; walks and talks like a girl. Girl avoids mother, wants to be different from mother; imitates father; doesn't like to play with girls; doesn't like "feminine" activities; walks and talks like a boy.	Does not recognize that he is a member of his family—rejects family, "searches" for a family to belong to. Cannot identify with father or mother: seeks someone to identify with.

Chapter 5
Aspects of Development
—Phase Development

The movement a child shows in terms of his general developmental unfolding can be taken as another indication of his overall progression in development. Within the psychoanalytic developmental framework, the child is conceived of as passing through several phases in the course of his development from infancy to latency. Each phase is characterized by certain pleasure-seeking strivings and assertive-imposing strivings which extract from the outside world the satisfaction of the individual's needs. Each phase has its own tasks and its own masteries, as well as its own concerns, needs, and conflicts.

The child is expected to go through an oral phase, an anal phase, a phallic phase, and an oedipal phase before latency; and at each phase he is expected to show certain developmental landmarks and certain kinds of behaviors. It is also expected that there will be progression in the expression of the aggressive drive, the child learning to delay the expression of aggression and learning to express his aggression in ways acceptable to his family, peer group, and community.

Inferences can be made about progression in terms of the libidinal phases and in terms of the aggressive drive by looking at evidences of the needs dominating the child, the conflicts being encountered and mastered, his concerns and anxieties, the inhibition-expression of the libidinal and aggressive drives, and the libidinal-aggressive balance. There is movement toward fusing mastery of the environment with satisfaction of the individual's desires for pleasure.

Libidinal Phases

Each phase of development is represented by a central theme. The pleasures-gratifications of the child, his play and other activities, his character traits, and the symptoms that appear are all related to this theme. Thus, getting information about these areas and inferring the child's anxieties and conflicts can suggest the level of development the child has reached. Such information would include observations about the child's eating habits, sleeping habits, toileting habits, interest in various part of his body, problem behavior, assertive-aggressive behavior and affectionate behavior, and his reactions to the assertive-aggressive behaviors and affectionate behaviors of others.

The inability to accept the implications of each successive phase as it emerges, and the fears related to the feelings involved, may result in distortions in the emerging behaviors in each phase of development. The purpose being served by the uncharacteristic behavior is essentially denial or escape from the discomfort of conflict in the unfolding of the developmental process.

The pleasures and/or gratifications the child seeks or permits himself, as well as the exaggerations of these or the absence of what would be expected, are important considerations in assessing the child's current phase of development. Certain manifestations are associated with the oral phase, others with the anal, phallic, or oedipal phase. An expected manifestation may, however, be overly intense or defended against. Symptoms can be looked at as ways of handling anxiety or as inappropriate conflict solutions.

Infant: Birth to One-and-a-Half Years (Oral Phase)

Pleasures-Gratifications. During infancy and for some

time after that, stimulation of the mouth is most pleasurable — hence the word "oral." There is need for immediate gratification and tension reduction; and the tension of the infant is reduced mainly through the mouth — sucking, swallowing, exploring. Gratification is in the context of a nurturing, dependent relationship with "mother" or a mother surrogate. There is pleasure in eating. The infant is expected to have a good appetite, good digestion, and little vomiting. He has pleasure in sucking, and he becomes increasingly able to give himself gratification by thumb- or finger-sucking or sucking other objects in moderation. He also finds pleasure in mouthing or oral exploring and eventually in biting and chewing.

Although oral activities are most pleasurable for the infant, there is also pleasure during this phase in body contact and body care — being held, cuddled, stroked, handled. There is pleasure in his own body functioning — urinating and defecating; there is pleasure in the use of his musculature — the movements of his body or arms or legs, and later the movements in turning, sitting, crawling, walking, and perhaps even some rhythmical movements such as rocking or swaying; and there is pleasure from the natural rhythm of sleeping-waking, falling asleep easily and sleeping well.

Theme. The basic theme of the oral phase is need-gratification. The "mother" is seen as need-gratifying and tension-reducing. The presence of the "mother" is linked with gratification and with protection against internal tension. The characteristic anxiety of the very young child, therefore, revolves around the loss of the "mother," the caretaking person. There is anxiety about being abandoned, being deprived. On an unverbalized level, the infant's questions are: "Will I be cared for or neglected?" "Will I get oral satisfaction or oral deprivation?" "Will there be constancy of the mother or loss? "Will there be a rhythm of tension-and-release or will there be chronic, unrelieved tension?"

Play. In his play, a child may elaborate on his current anxieties, concerns, and conflicts, and may express his impulses. Thus, the infant may engage in "oral" play, such as playing at being fed or feeding. The young child may play he is making food or giving food to someone else, or even feeding a baby. There may be play at biting others or devouring others or play at being bitten or devoured. There may be play that food is taken away and brought back; or that people or things will be "lost" and then found again. At this age, peek-a-boo is a favorite activity, as is dropping an object and having someone else retrieve it.

Character Traits. "Character traits" are a result of the drive discharge, the child's defense against anxiety aroused by the drive and his mode of relating to others. The character traits are the relatively fixed ways of relating himself to the world and to other people. They are also related to the phases of development. Thus, it is assumed that looking at the child's behaviors with others to determine his characteristic ways of relating to them can provide a basis for making inferences about the expression of his drives, his concerns, and his conflicts; and ultimately an inference about his developmental status can be made.

The newborn infant is passive, needing to be given to. He is dependent on others for his physical and emotional needs, although he gradually makes attempts to become independent. In order to be "fed," he may at times be demanding and egocentric. He is receptive to what is given to him and may be compliant as a way of getting his needs met. And, he is trusting in the expectation that his needs *will* be met and he will be taken care of. If he experiences prolonged tension and the caretaking person is not there, the child may become overwhelmed with anxiety.

Traits such as passivity, dependence, receptivity, compliance may continue long beyond infancy; they are, however, considered "oral" character traits, since they are primarily associated with this phase of development. An "oral" child may "give up easily" and look to others in a helpless way to be symbolically "fed." Other indications of concern about being taken care of include clinging behavior and much effort put into trying to please others. On the other hand, incorporating, devouring, and engulfing characteristics are also considered "oral," since they are associated with this phase, too. Such a child may seem difficult to satisfy, always demanding more, and complaining about what he is given.

Symptoms. The child's direct zonal expressions and pleasures, as well as the exaggerations of these or the denial or absence of what would be expected, may suggest some of the child's concerns or conflicts. For example, a child may be a finicky eater or an overeater; he may have extreme food preferences or avoidances; he may indulge in excessive sucking (finger, thumb, or other objects), biting, chewing, or oral exploring.

Other "oral" children may give the impression of insatiability with complaints of not getting enough (food, attention, gifts) or of not being treated fairly. Or, in contrast, in cases where the mother has not met the needs of the child, the child may have "turned away" from mother and may appear precociously independent, or may have "turned to" others as substitutes for mother — adults such as father or teacher.

In addition, the child's sleeping and resting habits can be noted. Much wakefulness, bad dreams, or being too agitated to rest may be indications of some anxiety. And exaggerations of "oral" character traits and repetitive "oral" play may be considered as symptoms of the child's concerns and conflicts.

Developmental Progression. Although a child may show oral manifestations, oral play, or oral character traits, any of these alone do not necessarily indicate the overall level of a child's developmental progression, since what is observable might be "left over" from the earlier phase. Also, it should be noted that the same symptoms or the same behavior may have many different meanings; they may, in fact, have different meanings for a given child at different times in his life.

Thus, any specific behavior or specific characteristic of a child must be looked at and evaluated in its relation to the overall picture of developmental progression — as a small part of an integrated whole.

Toddler: One-and-a-Half to Three Years (Anal Phase)

Pleasures-Gratifications. Following the oral phase, the next phase of development focuses on the pleasure of the child in acquiring control of his bodily functions. The word "anal" refers to the capacity of the child to take over the control of his own body. Significant interactions with mother take place during toilet training, which may also become an emotional experience. In this phase, the child is interested in toileting in general, his own and others', and may show interest in looking at or touching his bowel movements, as well as interest in his own buttocks and those of others. But this is also the period when there is pleasure in acquiring control of other musculature — large muscles for climbing and running, small muscles for handling objects.

During this period, the child realizes there is a certain orderliness in what is being done. He becomes interested in schedules and learns to accept scheduled times for toileting, meals, and going to bed. He may become aware that there are certain rituals around these activities and in fact may even acquire his own rituals. As there is evolvement of the control system of his whole body, he makes efforts to be clean, punctual, and orderly.

Theme. The basic theme of the anal phase is body control and the evolvement of a control system. There are such unverbalized questions as, "Can I exercise control over myself *and* my environment, or will I *be* controlled by others and/or by environmental factors?" "Can I control myself or will I *lose* control?" The theme of control as against loss of control is related to that of omnipotence/ helplessness.

Associated with his training to "be on schedule" and to follow prescribed rituals, there may be concern about being dirty or clean and about being disorderly or orderly.

There may also be the unverbalized question, "How much can I keep to myself and how much will be taken away?" Related to this are the themes of keeping or losing, keeping or giving away, and possession or loss of possession.

A new autonomy is being acquired by the child

exercising the right to say "No," and to push the mother away. However, if the child asserts himself, there is the risk that he will have to "pay the consequences." Thus, there is concern about getting hurt and hurting, being destroyed and destroying.

The characteristic anxieties are the fear of loss of control and fear of the loss of mother's love if he does not give in to her control.

Play. Children in the anal phase may play at toileting or have dolls play at toileting, soiling, and messing. In their play, children may express feelings about being dirty or clean, organized or disorganized, orderly or disorderly. "Anal" play may be disorganized and impulsive or its opposite, neat, organized, and repetitive.

"Bathroom" talk is common during this phase; and children may giggle and call each other names such as "Boo-boo," "Poo-poo," or "Dooty." Play with sand, clay, dirt, and paint are popular.

There may be repetitiveness in constructing something and knocking it down. At times, children may "collect" and guard particular toys or equipment. In playing, a child may have dolls hurt one another or have dolls getting hurt in various ways. Such play expresses the concerns of this phase.

Also, during the anal phase, there is much exploring of the environment, as part of the child's desire to control.

Character Traits. The character traits of the anal phase directly reflect the concerns of the child. During this phase, the child is making efforts to control himself and to do this on schedule. His efforts are directed toward being clean, punctual, and orderly. There is emphasis on "my" and "mine." At the same time, he is making efforts to protect himself against being controlled by others. Therefore, he may characteristically act defiant, obstinate, quarrelsome. Because he wants to "do it himself" — in his own way and at his own time — there is negativism. It is as if the child were saying, "I will do what I want when I want."

The child is reluctant to give up on demand what he has, and yet he may take pleasure in deciding himself to "give" a gift of his feces. There may be hoarding and stinginess, or there may be extravagance and wastefulness.

In his attempts to control others, the child may often show bossiness and domination. On the other hand, because of the concern about his own aggression and that of others (discussed in more detail below) and his concern about his own and others' destructiveness, as well as his concern about losing the love of his mother if he does not accept her control, there may be indecisiveness and ambivalence.

Symptoms. When the inherent drive to learn control of one's own body and the controlled use of the body is overwhelmed by fears regarding this drive, the behaviors characteristic of the anal phase of development are often distorted. They then represent not efforts toward growth but efforts toward denying the drive totally, or toward working through fears associated with the drives in excessive, exaggerated forms of activity. There may then appear compulsive, obsessive forms of behavior manifestly characteristic of the phase but differing from the characteristic in quality because of the difference in the need being served.

Distortions in behavior related to body functions — such as constipation, diarrhea, soiling, bedwetting — may be symptoms of the child's anxieties and may indicate some of his conflicts or concerns. This may also be true of his rituals and compulsions or obsessions.

Developmental Progression. Though a child may be observed to have anal manifestations, anal character traits, or "anal" play, any of these alone do not necessarily indicate the level of a child's development. They might be carried over from the anal phase to a later phase of development; and the same behavior or symptoms may have a variety of meanings at different times. Though they are primarily associated with the anal phase because of their association with this period, any specific anal behavior or characteristic of a child must be looked at in relation to the overall picture of his developmental progression.

Differentiating Stage: Three to Four-and-a-Half Years (Phallic Phase)

Pleasures-Gratifications. During the phallic phase, there is pleasure in "growing up" and becoming big and powerful. Related to this, the child gets pleasure also from being admired and pleasure from the attention and praise he receives. He enjoys "showing off" his abilities, achievements, and his attractiveness. As part of assessing and confirming his own development, he enjoys comparing himself with others — to see who is taller, faster, stronger, etc.

There is pleasure also in establishing his sexual identity. Simultaneously, there is interest in the differences between boys and girls; and related to this, there is interest in exhibiting one's own body and looking at the bodies of others, as well as in handling one's own body (masturbating, stroking the arms, playing with one's hair) and touching the bodies of others.

Theme. The basic themes of the phallic phase focus around "Who am I?" and How powerful am I?" There is concern about whether one is extraordinary-special-worthwhile or worthless, and concern about being admired or ridiculed. There is also concern about being bigger or smaller, stronger or weaker. With the evolving sexual identity, there is concern about being a boy or being a girl. And related to these concerns, the basic anxieties revolve around bodily damage (injury) and self-esteem.

Play. At the phallic phase, the child engages in much active, thrusting activity. Phallic children compete for attention and praise, as well as for equipment and materials. There is fun in water play and carpentry — sawing wood and putting creations together. Materials are used in a constructive way, and there is much emphasis on mastery in activity and on skills. There is simple dramatic play — the children playing real and unreal social roles such as doctor, teacher, ballerina, monster, superman — and much fun in "dressing up."

There is much curiosity about human anatomy and talk about the differences between males and females, as well as talk about being a boy or being a girl. Children play the game of "show" — which involves exposing the body or genitals to other children or urinating in front of them. There is much investigative play of other types also, taking things apart to see what is inside and how they work.

Character Traits. Phallic character traits include being competitive — to be best, biggest, strongest, prettiest, most loved, most admired, etc.; exhibitionistic — admiring oneself, bragging-boasting, "showing off"; being assertive and forceful. The phallic child actively seeks attention, takes pride in his accomplishments, and wants praise for his performances. The phallic boy makes efforts to be "masculine," and the phallic girl makes efforts to be "feminine."

Symptoms. Exaggerations of any of the above behaviors, or denials and absence of the expected behaviors and interests, would suggest some concerns or conflicts in the child and could be taken as symptoms. This would include excessive masturbation or denial of pleasure in, and avoidance of, touching parts of one's own body. It would also include excessive exhibitionism (and clowning as a distortion of exhibitionism) or, as a reaction against exhibitionism, great shame or modesty about one's own body, extreme neglect of oneself, being extremely shy rather than "showing off." There may be intensive interest in and prolonged attention to boy-girl differences and excessive looking at the bodies of others or avoidance of looking at the bodies of others.

Other symptoms in the phallic phase would be excessive concern about bodily harm or breakage, and phobias (e.g., dogs, heights, thunder).

Because of the concerns or conflicts, boys may deny their masculinity or may show exaggerated masculinity, and girls may deny their femininity or show exaggerated femininity. Because of his doubts, the child may constantly exhibit himself and seek attention and praise. Or, he may show the opposite traits — not daring to assert himself or show off or seek attention — seeming to be extremely shy and retiring instead.

Also, the avoidance of phallic types of play and activities might be taken as symptomatic of the child's concerns and conflicts.

Developmental Progression. A child may show phallic manifestations, phallic play, and phallic character traits, and yet any of these alone may not necessarily indicate the level of his development. Though certain activities and interests and behaviors are generally associated with this phase, any specific variable must be looked at in relation to the overall picture of developmental progression to understand its meaning for the child.

Family Integration: Four-and-a-Half to Six Years (Oedipal Phase)

After the child has achieved sexual identity — i.e., he is a boy or she is a girl, with father as man and mother as woman — he has to take the next step of integrating his new identity within the context of the family picture, and this leads to the Oedipal constellation. There is then both the need to identify with the same-sex parent (as there had been in the phallic phase) and at the same time the need to make a special alliance with the opposite-sex parent, and this leads to conflict. This conflict is necessary for the working-through of the child's relationships with both parents. Through this, the child establishes a sense of guilt for wishes and needs that are inappropriate and that do not take into account the rights of others — mother's and father's roles with each other. Therefore, during the Oedipal phase, there may be a great deal of conflict which may be expressed in fears, nightmares, sleep disorders.

Pleasures-Gratifications. During the Oedipal phase, the child experiences pleasure in identifying with the same-sex parent — in likes and dislikes, mannerisms, physical movements, and physical activities. At the same time, he enjoys contact with the opposite-sex parent and flirts with and "tries to win" that parent.

The child in the Oedipal phase also finds much pleasure in achieving, solving problems, and mastering difficulties.

Theme. The basic theme of the Oedipal phase is the romance of the opposite sex. Related to this may be concern about being like the same-sex parent, competing with the same-sex parent, and succeeding and replacing him by winning the opposite-sex parent. Because of the child's concerns about being like the same-sex parent and yet competing with him for the opposite-sex parent and possibly even replacing him, the themes focus also around persevering or "giving up" and not daring to succeed; loving the same-sex parent or wanting to get rid of him; being a parent.

Play. During the Oedipal phase, much time is spent in family play — "playing house." The boy usually plays "father" and the girl "mother," but not always. Family roles are easily shifted at this age. There are questions about marriage, and the child may propose marriage to either father or mother. The child is interested in the relationship between mother and father, though at times he may object to his parents being together. There is pleasure in doing things together wih the same-sex parent and pleasure in physical play with the opposite-sex parent.

There are also questions about where babies come from and how babies get out of the mother's stomach. There may be questions about the babyhood of the parents. At times there may be requests for a baby brother or a baby sister and even talk about having a baby "when I grow up."

Though questions about sex differences and babies may have been raised earlier, at this time the same questions have greater significance.

Continuing from the phallic phase, there may be sex play with other children, with much looking at one another and touching.

During the Oedipal phase, there is often complex dramatic play in small groups, as well as interest in small-group games. In addition, children in this phase are broadening their interests outside the family and want to learn more about their neighborhood and the larger community — to visit places, talk to people, see sights.

Character Traits. The Oedipal child is characteristically cooperative, friendly and responsive. He is usually charming and appealing. He may be seductive, flirtatious, and even manipulative with the opposite sex; at the same time he may compete with the same sex, then appease, and continue alternating between competing and appeasing.

Symptoms. If there is a disturbance during the Oedipal phase, the child may regress to earlier phases and may, for example, begin to show excessive oral behaviors or such behaviors as wetting his pants and his bed.

There may be excessive guilt during this phase because of the child's incestuous and murderous wishes, and the child may show excessive fear of males or fear of females. As a reaction to his destructive wishes, the child may show great fear of leaving a parent. Also, because of his own desires and fantasies, the child may develop a fear of growing up to be a "bad man" or a "bad woman."

Indications of the concerns and conflicts of the Oedipal phase would include acting in such a way as not to identify with the same-sex parent and to emphasize the differences from the same-sex parent or to exert great effort to appear better than the same-sex parent. There may be avoidance of the opposite-sex parent because of the "danger" of being involved with that parent. And, related to this, there may be inhibition of any hint of flirtatiousness or seductiveness with the opposite-sex parent. There may be fear of the consequences if he competes with the same-sex parent and succeeds in replacing that parent or defeating him.

Not only would it be symptomatic if the child avoided and rebuffed the opposite-sex parent, but also if the child were self-defeating in his relations with the opposite-sex parent; or if there were exaggerated seductiveness with the opposite-sex parent.

There would be questions also if the child were constantly challenging and then appeasing the same-sex parent.

Developmental Assessment Outline

Behavioral references of the libidinal phases are available to and can be noted by teachers and other child-care workers, and an estimate can then be made as to the child's progression in phase development.

The items included in the Assessment Outline of Early Child Development referring to the libidinal phases of development were extracted from what had been included in the intensive, comprehensive clinical study of the nonclinical children in the community nursery schools. However, it had been found that taking these particular items together could result in a valid and reliable gross indication of the child's current libidinal status.[1]

Aggressive Drive

In addition to the progression through the libidinal phases, it is assumed, within the psychoanalytic developmental framework, that there is progression in the expression of the aggressive drive. In some situations, the aggressive strivings are clearly seen when they lead to destructiveness. However, aggressive strivings are part of everyday, normal functioning; and the assertive-aggressive strivings are fused with the pleasure-seeking strivings as the child increases his capacity to integrate his drive demands with the demands of the environment.

There is movement from showing uncontrolled aggression to aggression being bound so that it is manifested both verbally and in action in ways socially acceptable to the child's family and community.

During the *oral phase,* the infant expresses his aggression in expressing his wants, making demands, imposing himself on his world to get what he wants, grabbing, "devouring," and biting. There is no consideration for others. Nor would we expect it at this early age. The infant reacts to restraint, delay of gratification, inhibition

---

[1]See Appendix B for discussion of validity and reliability.

of his activity, or to the aggression of others by crying, yelling, and striking out.

In the *anal phase,* the expression of aggression is seen in the child energetically going after what he wants and trying to reach his goals. There is obvious determination in his assertive-aggressive strivings. He can usually control his aggression to some extent, though occasionally he "loses control." His aggression may at times come out in trying to control others and trying to "shape" the environment to his desires. His reaction to others' aggression is immediate and short-lived. He may use language, such as scolding others or criticizing them; or he may shove others, get into a tug-of-war, or hit; or he may just cry. Assertive-aggressive strivings may come out also in attempts to dominate others or to force them to perform certain actions.

During this stage, the child may have difficulties with impulse control. Since there is little internal control of his own aggression, he must rely on external controls and on external support. His fear of punishment and of loss of love, as well as the developing fear of bodily injury, result in the aggression becoming modulated. However, throughout this phase, the child experiences much ambivalence and swings between "love" and "hate" for mother and other members of the family.

By the *phallic phase,* the child has modulated the expression of aggression and is able to express his assertive-aggressive strivings in moderate amounts and in socially acceptable ways — in most situations. He can assert himself when it is appropriate, pursue his own needs and get his wants satisfied. Also, he can show anger when it is appropriate. He can compete with other children for materials, favors, and attention. Often he competes with others through fantastic exaggeration and boasting. At times, the aggression may come out in achievement striving.

In our society, girls are more likely than boys to restrain their aggressive impulses, in an effort to please mother and meet mother's demands for what is considered "proper" for little girls. Yet, if there is massive inhibition of aggression and a turning of this aggression against the self, a child may develop masochistic tendencies.

By the time children are in nursery school, there is usually more social use of the aggressive drive. Occasionally, there may be strong outbursts of destructive tendencies — toward "bad" things, toward other children who have failed to share desired toys or materials, or toward other children who have attacked first. However, in general the aggressive drive is channeled into expressions acceptable to the peer group — pushing, poking, tickling, verbal provocation, laughing.

At the same time, the child in the phallic phase is able to express affection easily, both verbally and in action, and to respond to the expression of affection by others. He is also beginning to develop the capacity for sympathy and empathy.

By the *Oedipal phase,* the child is able to maintain more or less satisfying relations with others and still get what he wants. The assertive-aggressive strivings are more ego-oriented; they may come out in a show of initiative, in competitiveness, in efforts to develop his own autonomy and individuality, or in attempts to master the environment or to take some kind of "social action." By this phase, the child can be helpful to others and may even show some altruism.

The response of the Oedipal child to aggression by others is increasingly verbal and decreasingly physical. There may be insistence on compromise and mutual adjustments — though in our culture it appears that girls are more likely than boys to be peacemakers and compromisers.

In order to assess a child's aggressive drive, it is necessary to have information about his ways of expressing aggression, his ability to assert himself with others, and his ability to achieve his own goals. An observer can note how much aggression is expressed by the child and in what ways — for example, whether it is expressed primarily in activity or in fantasy; whether there is active, spontaneous expression or there is expression only in reaction to someone else's aggression or there is minimal expression. Related to this, an observer can also note whether the child is able to express affection to others, his ways of expressing positive feelings, and the kinds of response he evinces to the show of affection by others — since it has been found that children who are able to show affection and friendly behaviors are also the ones who are more likely to be able to show aggressive behaviors as well.[2]

Some children may not be able to show any aggression and are therefore unable to get what they want. They make little effort to master the environment, do not impose themselves on the world, but just "take in" and are passive and wait for others to give them what they desire. They may turn their aggression on themselves in which event symptoms may consist of accident proneness, self-inflicted injuries, or psychosomatic disorders. Such children may deny their own wants and pleasures, and they may appear primarily superego-oriented rather than ego-oriented (see the discussion in Chapter 6 on Superego Development). There may be excessive generosity and concern for others as a reaction formation to mask aggression.

With some children, the aggression may come out in devious ways, such as passive resistance, or dawdling, "accidentally" hurting others, or being destructive. With other children, fantasy may be the only way they can express their aggression.

On the other hand, some children may show so much aggression that it interferes with interpersonal relationships, and the child is not able to get the responses he wants from others.

Marked aggression that is externally directed, such as in cruelty, destructive behavior, and sadistic behavior, would raise questions about the child's developmental progression, as would insufficient aggression and inhibi-

[2]See Ruediger Schroeer and Dorothy Flapan, "Assessing Aggressive and Friendly Behaviors in Young Children," *Journal of Psychology,* 77:193–202, 1971; and Ruediger Schroeer and Dorothy Flapan, "Aggressive and Friendly Behaviors of Young Children from Two Social Classes," *Child Psychiatry and Human Development,* 2:32–41, 1971.

tion of assertive-aggressive strivings because of inner conflicts or fears.

Some children show only aggression and show no affection or friendly behavior. This is in contrast to other children who are overly affectionate or searching for affection and who show anxiety about the possible loss of love; or children who are uneasy about any expression of affection and show embarrassment or self-consciousness when it is necessary to be affectionate or receive affection.

Thus, conflict would be suggested if there were little effort by a child to master his environment, if there were constriction of initiative and/or denial of his own pleasures, if there were inhibition or restriction of any demonstration of affection.

In the longitudinal research study of nonclinical children, it had been found that the content of the child's play, his fantasies, his overt expressions of aggression and affection, as well as his lack of assertive-aggressive behavior and affectionate behavior, and his responses to the aggression and affection of others, can be noted and reported by teachers and child-care workers, even though these variables are not customarily mentioned or emphasized in reports about children.

The items included in the Assessment Outline of Early Child Development referring to the expression of and response to aggressive behaviors and affectionate behaviors were extracted from what had been included in the more extensive and comprehensive material in the research study of the nonclinical children. However, these items, taken together, give a valid and reliable gross indication of the current developmental status of the child's aggressive drive.[3]

---

[3]See Appendix B for discussion of validity and reliability.

Criteria for Assessing
PHASE DEVELOPMENT

Phase	Characteristic, expected, typical	Pleasures, Gratifications Uncharacteristic, unexpected, untypical, pathological	
		Ranging from:	To:
1. Infant: birth to 1½ (Oral Phase)	Able to find satiation-pleasure in eating, sucking, oral exploring or mouthing, biting, chewing, kissing. Good appetite, good digestion. Little vomiting. Able to give self gratification, e.g., thumb- or finger-sucking, sucking pacifier, toys. Pleasure from the natural rhythm of sleeping-resting. Pleasure in body functions. Pleasure in use of musculature — movements of body, arms, legs; turning, sitting, crawling.	Great indulgence in oral behaviors — voracious, gluttonous eating; continues frequent bottles beyond usual age of weaning; extensive oral exploring. Frequent and prolonged thumb-or finger-sucking, sucking other objects, mouthing. Frequent demands for body contact, being held. Extended periods of sleeping — "too much" sleeping, as if to avoid the world, escape. Much biting, grinding teeth, spitting, drooling.	No pleasure from eating — poor appetite, finicky eater, eats very little, habitually vomits. "Rejects" food. No attempts to give self gratification when it is lacking in the situation — does not show the expected oral exploring or mouthing, sucking, etc. No pleasure from body contact; avoids body contact; pushes away when held or cuddled. Resists going to sleep; restlessness in sleep; bad dreams; wakefulness. "Fights" sleep.
2. Toddler: 1½ to 3 (Anal Phase)	Pleasure in acquiring control of own body functions — urinating, defecating. Pleasure in use of musculature, large and small, and in acquiring control — climbing, walking, handling objects.	Toileting (and/or eating and/or sleeping) used as a statement vs. object ("I won't because you want me to") or as source of contention, rather than for pleasure. Anal zone unduly eroticized. Asking to be wiped after toileting; not wiping self well. Diarrhea (no control). Aggressive use of wetting or soiling (because disappointed in mother or suffering object loss). Excessive use of musculature — hyperactive, reckless. Frequent soiling, bed-wetting, pants-wetting.	No pleasure from body functions. Denies pleasure for self. Holding in — constipation. Excessive control. Disgust with body functions as reaction formation. Extremely clean and fussy with regard to body functions. Restricted use of musculature. Restricted in activity, cautious. Overly compulsive re toileting and/or cleanliness. Overly shy about excretory functions and procedures.

3. Differentiating Stage: 3 to 4½ (Phallic Phase)	Able to find pleasure in masturbation, playing with genitals, handling other parts of own body, e.g., playing with hair, stroking arm. Enjoyment of being nude, exhibiting self, "showing off." Pleasure in "poking," "piercing." Enjoyment of dressing up, looking handsome/pretty.	Frequent and prolonged masturbation — as reassurance and/or for comfort; intensive handling of own body or hair — "I can't stop." Excessive nudity; excessive exhibiting of self — to get attention or as reassurance against own doubts. Buffoonery or clowning as distortion of exhibitionism — "showing off" displaced from asset to defect. Excessive attempts to get attention. Constantly wanting to dress up, "look handsome/pretty," as reassurance against own doubts.	Denies self pleasure of masturbation; avoids handling own body. Inhibition of masturbation. Inhibition of nudity — not wanting to be seen in the nude. Excessive modesty — as reaction formation of exhibitionistic tendencies. Shame re body. Reaction against exhibitionism appears as neglect of dress and/or hair. Avoids attention. May be "bored" as a result of suppressing masturbation or fantasies re masturbation.
4. Family Integration: 4½ to 6 (Oedipal Phase)	Pleasure in exploring; in achievement; in mastering difficulties; in solving problems; in coping with novel situations. For boys: pleasure in "masculine" activities; in being "a little man," in identifying with father, in flirting with women and girls. For girls: pleasure in "feminine" activities; in being "a little woman," a "little mother," in identifying with mother, in flirting with men and boys.	"Pushes" self to achieve — to overcome own doubts. "Pushes" self to master difficult situations. "Pushes" self to explore; to solve problems. For boys: "pushes" self to engage in masculine activities, to prove masculinity; "pushes" self to be "a little man." Avoids all feminine activities. Exaggerated interest in masculinity. Excessive flirting with females. For girls: "pushes" self to engage in feminine activities to prove femininity; "pushes" self to be "a little woman," "a little mother." Avoids all masculine activities. Exaggerated interest in femininity. Excessive flirting with males.	Inhibits exploring, achieving, succeeding in difficult situations. Minimal pleasure in achievement, in exploring. For boys: avoids masculine activities; engages in feminine activities. Inhibits flirtatiousness with females. For girls: avoids feminine activities; engages in masculine activities. Inhibits flirtatiousness with males.

Criteria for Assessing
PHASE DEVELOPMENT

Phase	Characteristic, expected, typical	Themes and/or Central Issues	
		Uncharacteristic, unexpected, untypical, pathological	
		Ranging from:	To:
1. Infant: birth to 1½ (Oral Phase)	Concern about object being there — losing the caretaking person, being abandoned, being left alone (fear of annihilation due to loss of caretaking object). Concern about being given care — being neglected. Concern about being satisfied — being deprived; getting his share — not getting his share; devouring — being devoured.	Intense concern about losing the caretaking person, being abandoned — "I can't be without you" — panic when caretaking person out of sight. Intense concern about being given care — continually needing and demanding care; being greedy, seeing others as unfair. Intense concern about being satisfied — deprived; getting his share; "taking in." Intense anxiety about being devoured.	No bond established with the caretaking person; little interest in presence or absence of the object. Little expectation of being given care; child has "given up," is apathetic, uninvolved. Indifferent to satisfaction; may even "reject" satisfaction. Swings between extremes of demanding satisfaction and care, and exaggerated indifference.
2. Toddler: 1½ to 3 (Anal Phase)	Concern whether can control others or will be controlled by others (omnipotence-helplessness). Concern about giving in to others. Concern whether will lose love of objects (if say no); concern about pleasing authority (fear of criticism and punishment). Concern whether can establish own control system, can control self or will "lose control." Includes concern about cleanliness-dirtiness, orderliness-disarray,	Intense concern about being controlled by others; has to control them to avoid being controlled. Intense concern about losing love of object — continually seeking reassurance, trying to please, behaving so as not to incur any criticism. Extreme concern about losing control of self — becomes overcontrolled, rather than admit does not want to control self. Great concern about cleanliness-	Fearful of controlling others; tries to get others to control him. Fearful of showing concern about losing love of object. Goes to opposite extreme — acts as if does not want love, is unconcerned about pleasing. Fights against controlling self — appears to lack control of self; will not control self. Swings between extremes of overcontrol and lack of control.

Phase	Characteristic, expected, typical	Uncharacteristic, unexpected, untypical, pathological	
		Ranging from:	To:
	keeping-losing, aggression (hurting — getting hurt, destroying — being destroyed).	dirtiness, orderliness-disorderliness, keeping (hoarding), aggression by self or others (hurting others or getting hurt).	
3. Differentiating Stage: 3 to 4½ (Phallic Phase)	Concern about being extraordinary (special) or worthless, being admired-ridiculed; concern about size (being bigger-smaller), about strength (being powerful—strong or weak — vulnerable); concern about being attractive-unattractive. For *boys*: concern about male attributes, intactness and damage to body, castration, appearance as a boy; concern about *being a boy*, own worth as a boy. For *girls*: appearance as a female attributes; appearance as a girl; concern about *being a girl*, own worth as a girl.	As reaction to feeling worthless, great emphasis on being special, being admired (with fear of being ridiculed). As reaction to feeling small and weak, great emphasis on being big and strong and powerful. Great preoccupation with being attractive, admired, lovable. As reaction to concern about body-damage, castration, takes risks unnecessarily. For *boys*: intense concern about masculinity and efforts constantly to show masculinity; anxiety about being castrated and constant anticipation of being castrated and protective maneuvers to prevent castration. For *girls*: intense concern about femininity and efforts constantly to show femininity. Or, resigns self to "second-class" status and accentuates worthlessness as a girl.	Denial of special worth — may appear as overly modest; may act in ways to prove worthlessness. Fear of being big and strong, so emphasizes smallness and weakness and vulnerability. Lack of interest in appearance; or going to the opposite extreme and denying any interest in appearance. Denies desire to be lovable — acts unlovable. For *boys*: denial of interest in own maleness; appears unmasculine. For *girls*: denial of interest in being feminine; appears unfeminine. Denial of "second-class" status as a girl and efforts to show she is more worthy than a boy; constantly competing with boys.

Phase	Characteristic, expected, typical	Uncharacteristic, unexpected, untypical, pathological	
		Ranging from:	To:
4. Family Integration: 4½ to 6 (Oedipal Phase)	For *boys*: concern about being like or different from father; about competing with father for mother and competing with mother for father; concern about succeeding in competing with father as a male, persevering, or giving up because dare not succeed; concern about replacing father; concern about loving-getting rid of father. For *girls*: concern about being liked or different from mother; about competing with mother for father and competing with father for mother; concern about succeeding in competing with mother as a female, persevering, or giving up because dare not succeed; concern about replacing mother; concern about loving-getting rid of mother. For both boys and girls: concern about sex, reproduction, marriage.	For *boys*: because doubts he is like father, intense concern to prove he is like father; intense competition with father; great concern that mother prefers him to father; intense concern about being better than father. For *girls*: because doubts she is like mother, intense concern to prove she is like mother; intense competition with mother; great concern that father prefers her to mother; intense concern about being better than mother. For *both*: overly concerned about sex, reproduction, marriage.	For *boys*: fear of being like father; tries to be different from father; fear of consequences if competes with father and succeeds; strong need to fail. Avoids mother because of the danger, or avoids father. Appears to have great fear of females and/or males. Cannot let self replace father. For *girls*: fear of being like mother; tries to be different from mother; fear of consequences if competes with mother and succeeds; strong need to fail. Avoids father because of the danger, or avoids mother. Appears to have great fear of males and/or females. Cannot let self replace mother. For *both*: absence of any interest in sex, reproduction, marriage.

Criteria for Assessing
PHASE DEVELOPMENT

Play and Interests

Phase	Characteristic, expected, typical	Uncharacteristic, unexpected, untypical, pathological
1. Infant: birth to 1½ (Oral Phase)	Play at feeding and being fed; being "baby," being taken care of; eating, swallowing, devouring and being eaten, swallowed, devoured; biting others and being bitten. Play at losing and finding (as in peek-a-boo games, or hiding and finding toys, or dropping things and having them returned). Play at sleeping.	Intensive interest and/or prolonged play re feeding and being fed; being "baby"; devouring and/or being devoured. Intensive interest and/or prolonged play re losing and finding — people, things, toys.	Avoidance of playing "baby"; playing at devouring or being devoured. "Panic" or other strong reaction in refusing such play. Little interest in surroundings — in touching, handling.
2. Toddler: 1½ to 3 (Anal Phase)	Sublimation of anal and urethral preoccupation in painting, finger painting, modeling clay, water play, play with sand, other "messing," activities or dirtying activities. "Toilet" play. Play at being angry; at "destroying"; at hurting and getting punished or being hurt (e.g., with dolls). Play at being witch, devil, monster. Collecting materials and toys; some hoarding. Play at being angry; scolding. Interest in bowel movements; in toileting — his own and others; in buttocks — his own and others.	Intensive interest and/or prolonged play with water, sand, clay, paint, "messing," "dirtying." Extreme messiness, dirtyness. Great amount of "toilet" talk, "toilet" play. Much angry play; much destructive play; much hurting play. Destructive with materials and toys. Much teasing play, scaring other children. Extreme wastefulness. Intensive interest and/or prolonged attention to body functions; much concern expressed and much discussion of them.	Avoidance of painting, finger painting, modeling clay, water play, play with sand, "messing" activities or "dirtying" activities. Extreme cleanliness and orderliness. Denial of body functions and avoidance of any "toilet" talk or "toilet" play. Cannot let self engage in any angry play or any destructive play. Inhibits expression of anger even in play. "Saves" materials, is cautious, thrifty, in their use; much hoarding.

Phase	Characteristic, expected, typical	Uncharacteristic, unexpected, untypical, pathological	
		Ranging from:	To:
3. Differentiating Stage: 3 to 4½ (Phallic Phase)	Interest in looking at others' genitals, touching; showing own genitals to others; watching others dressing, bathing, nude. Questions about differences between boys and girls. As sublimation of sexual curiosity, enjoys taking things apart to see what is inside, what makes them work. Investigative play. For *boys*: engages in boy-type play — play at shooting, stabbing, warring; play with cars and trucks and airplanes; play at social roles, such as policeman, fireman, milkman, and other culturally emphasized roles; play with both sexes. For *girls*: engages in girl-type play — play at mothering and homemaking; play with dolls; play at social roles of ballerina, nurse, teacher, and other culturally emphasized roles.	Great interest in and/or prolonged attention to looking at others' genitals, showing own; watching others dressing, bathing, nude. Continuous and/or prolonged questioning about differences between boys and girls. Constantly taking things apart; investigative play. For *boys*: great emphasis on boy-type play and avoidance of *all* activities considered characteristic of girls. For *girls*: great emphasis on girl-type play and avoidance of *any* boy-type play; avoidance of *all* activities considered characteristic of boys.	Denial of *any* interest in genitals. Avoidance of *any* looking at others' and/or showing self. Extreme modesty. Denial of *any* sexual curiosity. Avoidance of questions about differences between boys and girls. Embarrassed by such discussions or references. For *boys*: avoidance of boy-type play; great interest in girl-type play and activities considered characteristic of girls. For *girls*: avoidance of girl-type play; great interest in boy-type play and activities considered **characteristic of boys.** **Little play at social roles — male or female.**

Phase	Characteristic, expected, typical	Uncharacteristic, unexpected, untypical, pathological	
		Ranging from:	To:
4. Family Integration: 4½ to 6 (Oedipal Phase)	Much time in family play — playing same-sex parent, most of the time; but sometimes playing child or opposite-sex parent. Some sex play. Talk about wanting to marry, about wanting to be a parent (father/mother). Girls play at being hostess, developing social skills; boys play at being guest. Questions about where babies come from; interest in taking care of a baby. Interest in exploring, learning. Interest in social activities of the group. Complex dramatic play. Interest in small-group games. Play at achieving, mastering difficulties, solving problems.	Practically all the time is spent in family play, to the exclusion of other kinds of play. Much sex play. Constant talk about wanting to marry. Excessive questioning about where babies come from. Intense interest in exploring, learning. Intense interest in the group. Forces self to enter and deal with difficult situations — in an effort to overcome own anxieties and doubts. For boys: great emphasis on always playing daddy; unwilling to take other roles in play. Constant talk about wanting to be a father. For girls: great emphasis on always playing mother; unwilling to take other roles in play. Constant talk about wanting to be a mother.	Avoidance of any family play. Avoidance of any sex play. Avoidance of any talk about marrying or about being a parent (father or mother). Uncomfortable in such discussions. Acts naive. Avoidance of any questions about where babies come from. Embarrassed by such talk. Denies interest in exploring, learning and/or avoids exploring-learning activities. Denies interest in social activities of the group and/or avoids group. Insists on setting up own individual play — extreme degree of independence and isolation.

Criteria for Assessing
PHASE DEVELOPMENT

Phase	Character Traits		
	Characteristic, expected, typical	Uncharacteristic, unexpected, untypical, pathological	
		Ranging from:	To:
1. Infant: birth to 1½ (Oral Phase)	Passive — in order to be given to. Receptive — to what is given. Dependent — for physical and emotional needs; some attempts to be independent. Wanting to be "fed" — demanding. Compliant — as a way to get needs met. Trusting — in expectation needs will be met and he will be taken care of.	Few attempts to become independent; fearful (anxious?) and therefore clinging for gratification and protection. Extremely passive and/or dependent. Extremely compliant, obedient, submissive, ingratiating — so as to be taken care of. Much whining.	As defense against passive wishes and fantasies, complains about being maltreated and discriminated against. Complains about not getting enough; wants what others have; sees others treating him unfairly. Always wants more, greedy, grabbing, unable to share, extremely demanding, insistent. Because disappointed in object or frustrated, has turned away and become precociously independent. *Cannot* let self be dependent, receptive, fed. Lack of trust; untrusting. Swings between being extremely independent and extremely demanding.
2. Toddler: 1½ to 3 (Anal Phase)	Emphasis on "me" and "mine." Attempts to control others. Some bossiness, some dominating. Efforts to protect self from being controlled by others. Negative, defiant, opposing, stubborn, obstinate. Teasing; quarrelsomeness. Ambivalent; indecisive. Efforts to be clean, orderly, punctual; to control self.	Extreme resistance to control by others. Extreme negativism, defiance, opposition, stubbornness, obstinacy, quarrelsomeness. Much bossiness; very dominating; very controlling of others. Much teasing; much insulting others. Easily feels insulted, hurt. Sadistic — seems to enjoy hurting others.	Unaggressiveness as indication of conflict with anal striving. Child presents too little trouble and difficulty for adults; will *not* permit self to be negative, defiant, stubborn, quarrelsome. *Must* agree. Masochistic — seems to enjoy being hurt. As reaction against wish to be bossy, dominate, control others

Phase	Characteristic, expected, typical	Uncharacteristic, unexpected, untypical, pathological	
		Ranging from:	To:
		Extreme ambivalence; extreme indecisiveness, e.g., clinging as expression of ambivalence and/or control rather than for protection. Will not be orderly, punctual, clean. Absence of self-control.	— lets self be bossed, dominated, controlled. Extremely orderly, punctual, clean. Overly self-controlled.
3. Differentiating Stage: 3 to 4½ (Phallic Phase)	Competing (to be best, biggest, strongest, most attractive, most loved); challenging others; bragging-boasting. Exhibitionistic — admiring self, proud of self. Seeking attention. Forceful, assertive, "thrusting" (girls not as forceful as boys). "Masculine" — active, aggressive, tough. "Feminine" — gentle, soft, socially skillful.	Extremely competitive most of the time; continually challenging others, bragging. Constantly exhibiting self, "showing self off"; constantly seeking attention of adults and/or other children by questioning, talking, performing, clowning, provoking. Great preoccupation with being attractive, admired, lovable. *Boys* show exaggerated masculinity as overcompensation for own fears and doubts (e.g., castration fear). *Girls* show exaggerated femininity in actions and dress.	Does not dare assert self — appears passive. Avoids competing, challenging. As reaction against wish to exhibit, is extremely retiring, shy. Avoids *any* exhibitionism. Avoids attention. Becomes embarrassed when given attention. Denies desire to be lovable — acts in unlovable ways to prove he/she is unlovable. *Boys* deny "masculinity" — cannot let self be active, aggressive, tough. *Girls* deny "femininity" — cannot let self meet cultural expectations, cannot let self be gentle; act more like a boy than a girl — tough, aggressive.

Phase	Characteristic, expected, typical	Uncharacteristic, unexpected, untypical, pathological	
		Ranging from:	To:
4. Family Integration: 4½ to 6 (Oedipal Phase)	Seductive, manipulating, "appealing." Responsive, friendly, cooperative. Charming with opposite sex (adults and children), flirtatious, coy. Competing with same sex (adults and children) and then often appeasing. Challenging same sex — establishing own sexual identity.	Extremely manipulative. Exaggerated seductiveness. Extremely flirtatious with all the opposite sex (adults and children). Unable to cooperate. Unfriendly, unresponsive. Constantly competing with same sex.	Self-defeating in any encounters with same sex (adults and children). Self-punishing. Avoids opposite sex — may rebuff them. Unable to compete with same sex. Overly cooperative, "too nice," too friendly, too responsive. Constantly appeasing same sex.

Criteria for Assessing
PHASE DEVELOPMENT

Phase	Characteristic, expected, typical	Symptoms and/or Problems	
		Uncharacteristic, unexpected, untypical, pathological	
		Ranging from:	To:
1. Infant: birth to 1½ (Oral Phase)	Oral autoerotic gratification — sucking thumb, finger, toys, etc; drooling, spitting, licking lips; sticking out tongue, rolling tongue. Occasional eating problems. Occasional sleep disturbances. Rocking, swaying, other rhythmical movements.	Continual eating problems — refusing to eat, vomiting, fussy eater, etc. Much biting self, others, toys, etc. Continual sleep disturbances, nightmares. Much rocking, head-banging. Much restless activity; "high." Frequent and prolonged crying. Excessive irritability.	Most of the time spent engaging in oral autoerotic behaviors such as sucking. Chronically depressed, dejected. Apathetic most of the time.
2. Toddler: 1½ to 3 (Anal Phase)	Needs some assistance after toileting, such as pulling up pants. Resists going to bed or resting. Needs special blanket or toy to sleep or rest. Some conflict over eating, dressing, etc. Compulsions, rituals, obsessions. Avoidance of or flight from anxiety-provoking situations. Magical thinking.	Frequent bed-wetting, pants-wetting, Diarrhea. Frequent soiling. Refuses to wipe self. Asks to be wiped after toileting. Chews things. Extreme and persistent anger, overly aggressive. Much destructive behavior. Extremely dirty, disorderly, wasteful.	Refuses to toilet except at home. Chronic constipation. Picks at fingers, scabs, nose. Bites fingernails; grinds teeth. Cannot express aggression toward others — turns it inward. Extreme cleanliness, orderliness, hoarding.

Phase	Characteristic, expected, typical	Uncharacteristic, unexpected, untypical, pathological	
		Ranging from:	To:
3. Differentiating Stage: 3 to 4½ (Phallic Phase)	Phobias, fears. Fears are realistic and/or age-appropriate. Fears as response to danger, to feelings of helplessness. Some fears about being hurt, about bodily damage. Some masturbation, handling or holding genitals, stroking skin, stroking or twisting hair.	Keeps fears hidden. Cannot admit fears or show fears. Maintains "brave front." Too few fears are observable. Denies fears. Severe nightmares or bad dreams. Frequent and prolonged masturbation. Excessive concern re being hurt, damaged.	Extensive and/or intensive phobias and fears, e.g., panic re cat or dog. Fears frequently interfere with functioning. Denial of any pleasure in own body. Inhibits any masturbation or autoerotic activity.
4. Family Integration: 4½ to 6 (Oedipal Phase)	Temporary regression to symptoms or problems of earlier phases. Some guilt re own wishes and fantasies.	Prolonged regression to earlier phases, e.g., soiling, wetting, excessive oral behaviors and activities.	Great fear of males and/or females. Great fear of leaving parent — as reaction against own destructive wishes. Excessive guilt. Fear of growing up to be a "bad" man or a "bad" woman.

Criteria for Assessing
PHASE DEVELOPMENT

Phase	Characteristic, expected, typical	Expression of Aggression	
		Uncharacteristic, unexpected, untypical, pathological	
		Ranging from:	To:
1. Infant: birth to 1½ (Oral Phase)	Expresses wants, makes demands, imposes self on world. No consideration for others. Grabs. Reacts to restraint with aggression: with crying, yelling, striking out. Also, reacts to interruption of activity and to delay of gratification. Can be diverted, placated. Oral aggression — "biting," "devouring."	Continually expressing wants, making demands. Maximally imposes self on environments; little effort to adjust to environment. Frequent displays of strong aggression — global, undifferentiated rage — for extended periods of time. Cannot be diverted, placated. Much oral aggression — biting, oral attacking, devouring.	Minimally imposes self on environment; usually tries to "adjust" self to demands of environment. Always tries to please, obey, comply. Extreme passivity. Undemanding. Helpless. Waits for others to give him what he desires or wishes. Seldom any display of aggression — even when it would be expected.
2. Toddler: 1½ to 3 (Anal Phase)	Anal aggressive. Swings between love and hate — ambivalence — libido and aggression not fused with each other. Enough aggression to go after what he wants and to reach goals. At times, aggressively controlling. Can usually control his own aggression — keep it within limits — though sometimes loses control. Tries to control others to some extent.	Extreme aggressivity. Aggression interferes with relations. Balance of love and hate swings toward hate, hostility, cruelty. Sadistic — much "hurting" others — insulting, teasing. Much hitting, kicking, scratching, throwing. Hurting by explosions of messy, destructive behavior. Outbursts of destruction. Uncontrolled aggression much of the time — destroys social relations. Great aggressiveness as reaction to fear.	Unaggressive. Cannot assert self. Reaction formation against sadistic impulses — overconcern re others' pains and wounds. Turns aggression on self. Accident-prone. Masochistic — much being hurt; easily feels insulted; sensitive to criticism. Hurting by keeping in, hiding feelings. Overcontrol of aggression. "Pacifism" as reaction to wish to attack or as expression of fear of being attacked.

Phase	Characteristic, expected, typical	Uncharacteristic, unexpected, untypical, pathological	
		Ranging from:	To:
3. Differentiating Stage: 3 to 4½ (Phallic Phase)	Phallic aggressive. In most situations, able to express aggression in moderate amounts and in socially acceptable ways (in words and/or in actions). Some consideration for others. Independent achievement strivings. Can compete with other children for toys, favors, attention. Can show anger when appropriate; can assert self; can pursue own ends and get wants satisfied. Aggression channeled into acceptable expressions — poking, tickling, verbal provocations, exaggeration. Girls less aggressive than boys. Girls more often than boys may express aggression in devious ways and/or in fantasy.	Competitiveness may be extremely aggressive. "Castrates." Noisy aggression as overcompensation for castration fear. Asserts self in extreme ways and/or attacks others. Fiercely pursues own ends. Marked aggression, externally directed, disrupts relations. Marked aggression is less typical of girls than of boys — but may come out by competing with boys, "castrating" boys.	Unable to show aggression directly, unable to assert self and/or unable to get what he wants. Inhibits aggression or expresses it in devious ways or in self-inflicted injuries. Psychosomatic disorders. Passive resistance, "accidentally" hurting others. Aggression expressed in fantasy rather than in activity. Girls are more likely to inhibit aggression than are boys.
4. Family Integration: 4½ to 6 (Oedipal Phase)	Balance between attempts to master (cope with) environment and attempts to satisfy own desire for pleasure (neutralization and fusion). Both the pleasure and the aggression have moved toward	Extreme emphasis on attempts to master environment. Manipulates aggressively. May manipulate by being seductive. Particularly aggressive toward same-sex parent.	Little or no effort to master environment, manipulate others. Constriction of initiative. More "superego"-oriented than ego-oriented or reality-oriented. Excessive generosity as reaction formation to mask aggression.

Little initiative; not enough aggression to reach goals; waits for help.

Phase	Characteristic, expected, typical	Uncharacteristic, unexpected, untypical, pathological	
		Ranging from:	To:
	reality. Pleasure principle giving way to reality principle. Ego-oriented, reality-oriented. Able to maintain satisfying relations with others and still get what he wants. Aggression may come out in show of initiative, in developing autonomy. Aggression may come out in attempts to master environment or to take "social action."		

Criteria for Assessing
PHASE DEVELOPMENT

Phase	Characteristic, expected, typical	Response to Aggression by Others Uncharacteristic, unexpected, untypical, pathological	
		Ranging from:	To:
1. Infant: birth to 1½ (Oral Phase)	Reacts immediately to aggression by others with crying, yelling, striking back.	Prolonged and intense reaction to felt aggression by others.	Passively accepts others' aggression. Does not defend self or respond with counteraggression. Usually turns to adult for help; or, may just whine helplessly.
2. Toddler: 1½ to 3 (Anal Phase)	Reacts to others' aggression, but shows some control of his response. May use language, may shove other, may cry. Reaction is immediate and short-lived. May scold or criticize or lecture other.	Reacts in extremely aggressive and angry way to any display of aggression by others. May bite, kick, scratch, inflict injuries, throw blocks or toys. Overreacts, cannot control self. May scream, yell, strike out physically.	Weak response to aggression. Made anxious or fearful by display of even moderate aggression. May run away in fear, show hurt withdrawal, cry, or stand immobilized.
3. Differentiating Stage: 3 to 4½ (Phallic Phase)	Easily tolerates moderate show of aggression by others. Takes it in stride. May respond by asserting self, by acting aggressive in words or actions but in socially acceptable ways. Girls are more likely than boys to respond in verbal ways.	Cannot tolerate any show of aggression by others; overreacts. May become either extremely physically aggressive or extremely verbally aggressive. Violent attack, challenge.	**Shows "superiority" by ignoring the aggression in obvious ways. May regress to passive, helpless acceptance of aggression.**
4. Family Integration: 4½ to 6 (Oedipal Phase)	Response to aggression by others is increasingly verbal. Insistence on compromise, justice, democratic process. Girls more likely than boys to be peacemakers.	Regresses to earlier ways of responding to aggression by others.	Extreme guilt and blames self for being cause of others' aggression. Excessively appeasing to aggressive one.

Criteria for Assessing
PHASE DEVELOPMENT

Phase	Characteristic, expected, typical	Expression of Affection Uncharacteristic, unexpected, untypical, pathological	
		Ranging from:	To:
1. Infant: birth to 1½ (Oral Phase)	Able to express some affection — by hugging, cuddling, kissing, stroking — to mother and maybe other family members.	Excessive show of affection; overly affectionate (continually hugging, kissing, touching, stroking others). Affection as a way of clinging for protection and gratification, for reassurance.	Shows only limited expression of affection, if any — only to mother or mother-substitute.
2. Toddler: 1½ to 3 (Anal Phase)	Able to express affection in actions, and sometimes verbally, to family members and an occasional friend of the family who is familiar.	Uses affection as a way of controlling others, as a way of being aggressive — e.g., hugging too hard. Excessive affection.	Inhibits or restricts demonstrations of affection. Very selective re persons toward whom shows affection. Uninterested in showing any affection. It is not that he inhibits affection he feels, but rather he does not *experience* affectionate feelings.
3. Differentiating Stage: 3 to 4½ (Phallic Phase)	Able to express affection verbally and in actions — to family members, teachers, and/or peers — in an easy and unselfconscious way.	Great show of affection. Indiscriminate re object of affection. May use affection in sexual way, in exhibitionistic way. Overly affectionate.	Uneasy about expressing any affection. Limited expression of affection. Show of affection may be accompanied by embarrassment, self-consciousness, silliness, clowning. May express affection only in indirect, devious ways. May express affection primarily in fantasy.

Phase	Characteristic, expected, typical	Uncharacteristic, unexpected, untypical, pathological	
		Ranging from:	To:
4. Family Integration: 4½ to 6 (Oedipal Phase)	Especially affectionate with parent of opposite sex and with other substitutes for this parent. Less affectionate with same-sex parent and with other substitutes for this parent.	Uses affection in extremely manipulative ways. Overly affectionate with opposite-sex parent and with substitutes for this parent. Unable to show any affection for same-sex parent or with substitutes for this parent.	Unable to be affectionate — especially with opposite-sex parent and with substitutes for this parent.

Criteria for Assessing
PHASE DEVELOPMENT

Phase	Characteristic, expected, typical	Response to Affection by Others Uncharacteristic, unexpected, untypical, pathological	
		Ranging from:	To:
1. Infant: birth to 1½ (Oral Phase)	Able to accept affection from mother and other family members. Responds to affectionate overtures. Enjoys being cuddled, kissed, hugged, stroked.	Overly responsive to affection — undiscriminating about who is giving it — as if "hungry" for it.	Unresponsive to affection — "as if numb." Cannot let himself be cuddled. Pushes out of person's arms or lap. Does not like to be kissed, hugged, handled.
2. Toddler: 1½ to 3 (Anal Phase)	Accepts affection in an easy way from family and familiar adults or children, and may even appear pleased by it. At times may refuse, as a way of showing he is in control of the situation.	Usually searching for affection; shows anxiety about the possible loss of affection. Asks for demonstrations of affection and for reassurance. If affection is shown, may respond by becoming overaffectionate. Seeks affection to counteract own ambivalence and negativism.	Uncomfortable about accepting affection from others and untrusting of their affection. Sees affection as attempt to control him. May reject or withdraw from all affectionate overtures from others. May be able to accept only limited expressions of affection from certain persons. Uninterested in and unresponsive to any affection from others. Does not look for affection or expect it.
3. Differentiating Stage: 3 to 4½ (Phallic Phase)	Responds to affection by peers, as well as by teacher and other familiar adults.	Affection accepted with embarrassment, self-consciousness, silliness, clowning, hyperactivity.	Too shy to respond to affection. May show uneasiness about others being affectionate.
4. Family Integration: 4½ to 6 (Oedipal Phase)	More responsive to affection from opposite-sex parent, or substitutes for that parent, than to affection from same-sex parent.	Overly responsive to affection from opposite-sex parent. Rejects any affection from same-sex parent.	Rejects affection from opposite-sex parent. Overly responsive to affection from same-sex parent.

Chapter 6
Aspects of Development
— Superego Development

The moral development of a child — or the development of his superego — is another aspect of developmental progression that is important to assess. The superego deals with the emerging values of the child, his capacity to differentiate between right and wrong, his anticipation of and reaction to punishment, and his guilt. "Superego" refers to the extent of the child's internalization of parental prohibitions and values, his adjustments to the social standards of his cultural group, the extent to which the child sees himself living up to his ego ideal, and the consequent positive or negative feelings about or attitudes toward himself.

Indices of Development

By getting information about the development of the child's ideas about "good" and "bad," and his capacity to differentiate "right" and "wrong," and by getting descriptions of the ways the child's behavior is affected by the presence or absence of an adult — that is, his need for external control, his dependence on external authority — and the child's response to discipline, rules, limits, directions, it is possible to make inferences about how much internalization there has been of the values of his family and community, and the extent to which an independent "code" of behavior is emerging.

By looking at a child's fantasies about, and/or his expectations of, punishment, as well as his reactions to disapproval and punishment, it is possible to infer something about the severity of his superego, his feelings of guilt, and his moral rigidity (or tolerance).

By observing the aspects of himself and the behaviors he is proud of or ashamed of, his standards and ideals for himself, the extent to which he sees himself living up to his own ideals, and his reaction to external evaluations such as praise or criticism, it is possible to get some indication as to the integration of the child's ego-ideal and self-esteem with his behavior.

Stages of Development

This aspect of development differs from other aspects of development in that there is no evidence of it in the infant. It is later in appearing than any of the other aspects of development.

In the oral stage of development, the infant does not yet "know" the difference between right and wrong, good and bad, which acts are approved and which disapproved, what he should do and what he should not do. He does not, in the beginning, anticipate punishment or have guilt. Nor does he yet have a "self" to have feelings about or an ego-ideal.

During the later part of the oral stage, but much more during the anal stage of development, the child learns in a gross way that some actions are considered good and some bad; that some ways of behaving are regarded as right and some wrong. He also learns which specific actions are approved and which disapproved by his parents, as well as what his parents think he *should* do or should *not* do. He knows that certain behaviors will be punished by the members of his family; he may, therefore, avoid such behaviors when others are around but may indulge in them when no adult is present. In these early stages of development, the child primarily relies on external criteria for evaluation of right and wrong, and relies on others to control his actions. These learnings, however, are precursors of the superego.

By the phallic stage of development, the child "knows" the difference between right and wrong, as defined by his family members and their social group; he "knows" what kinds of behaviors are approved and disapproved, rewarded and punished, by the adults; and he knows which behaviors are expected of, and considered appropriate for, a boy in our culture and which for a girl.

The child, by this stage, may be "good" and "act right" even though an adult is not present. He shows awareness or concern about goodness-badness in others. He may criticize "bad" children to the adult, or warn other children not to be "bad." He has positive feelings about himself when he is "good" and when he acts appropriately, and negative feelings about himself when he is "bad" or when he acts inappropriately. There are self-feelings of pride and of shame; and these self-feelings can be observed.

During the Oedipal stage of development, the child idealizes and identifies with his parents and wants to comply with their demands. An ego-ideal has begun developing. The "ego-ideal" refers to what an individual would like to be like — his ambitions for himself and his ideals for himself. His self-esteem is affected by how he sees himself measuring up to his ideals. Observations can be made of how he tries to maintain his self-esteem, what he does to keep his good opinion of himself, as well as what type of actions or situations lower his self-esteem. The child who achieves his own standards and sees himself as successful appears to others as a self-confident person, secure about his ability. He is usually proud of what he has done and takes pride in doing well.

Also, during the Oedipal phase, the child develops expectations of and fantasies about being "bad," and for the first time experiences feelings of guilt. The child may try to avoid punishment by blaming others, saying "it was an accident," promising "never to do it again" or by trying to atone for, or make up in some way for, wrongdoing. Thus, the superego takes over the role of the parent. It regulates the drives and inhibits drive expression through approval-disapproval.

It is expected that the Oedipal child will usually act in ways that he thinks are "good," whether or not an adult is present, and will usually follow the rules — though there may be occasional transgressions.

Symptoms

If a child is hypersensitive about what is right or wrong, overly strict with himself and/or others, overly concerned about "badness" in himself and/or others (moralistic) and *must* be good, this would be taken as an indication of his concerns and conflicts. He might also show anxiety about seeing himself as a "bad" person, "hating" himself; or his guilt might be expressed in fears and nightmares.

On the other hand, if a child acts to gratify infantile impulses (e.g., taking others' belongings) or acts antisocially, whether or not an adult is present, and does not seem to know the difference between right and wrong, this would be taken as an indication that the superego has not developed as expected, and thus would suggest that there is interference with development.

There would be some question also about children who set their standards for themselves unrealistically high, so that they cannot usually meet their own standards and therefore see themselves as unsuccessful. Such children seem insecure about their abilities and usually do not feel proud of their own work. Consequently, they show frequent shifts in self-feelings, influenced by the comments of others, especially authority figures.

Developmental Assessment Outline

To some extent, teachers have had experience in assessing this aspect of development. They are cognizant of the extent to which children respond or do not respond to rules and regulations, and cooperate or do not cooperate with the discipline of the school. They also have some awareness of which children "test" limits and which children are overly strict with themselves and with others. It has not been customary for teachers to examine the child's ideals for himself or his attitude toward himself. However, when the teachers were specifically asked for this information in interviews during the research study on nonclinical children attending community nursery schools, they were able to provide it.

As with the other aspects of development discussed above, the items included in the short assessment outline were extracted from what had been included in the more comprehensive clinical study of the nonclinical children. It had been found, however, that taken together these particular items resulted in a valid and reliable gross assessment of the child's superego development.[1]

[1]See Appendix B for discussion of validity and reliability.

Criteria for Assessing
SUPEREGO DEVELOPMENT

Phase	Characteristic, expected, typical	Emergence of Superego Uncharacteristic, unexpected, untypical, pathological	
		Ranging from:	To:
1. Infant: birth to 1½ (Oral Phase)	Does not yet "know" the difference between right and wrong, good and bad, which actions are approved and which disapproved, what he should do and what he should not do. Acts to gratify impulses, whether or not adult is present. May act "good" or "bad" depending on own impulses and desires. May act antisocially, take others' possessions, bite. Learning to respond when someone says "No." Learning inhibition of biting, grabbing.	Does not respond to "No." No inhibition of biting, grabbing, other antisocial actions.	Overresponds to "No" or to scolding or spanking. Withdraws into self. Becomes frightened and/or apathetic.
2. Toddler: 1½ to 3 (Anal Phase)	"Knows" in a gross way that some actions are considered good and some bad, some ways of behaving are regarded as right and some wrong. "Knows" which specific actions are approved and which disapproved by parents. "Knows" what parents think he should do and shou'd not do. Knows certain behaviors will be punished and	Does not comply with parents' requests or demands. Little guilt. "Tests" limits of adult. May deliberately provoke adults, e.g., by breaking rules. Acts in ways he thinks are "good" only when an adult is present; little capacity to decide right and wrong — does not "know" specific	Perceives parents as very powerful, supermoral, superhuman. Always acts in ways he thinks "good," even when adult is not present. Can never let himself do anything "wrong," or "bad." Has to follow rules. Great concern about badness in self and others. Very strong feelings about right and wrong. Much

Phase	Characteristic, expected, typical	Uncharacteristic, unexpected, untypical, pathological	
		Ranging from:	To:
	avoids these when others are around. Says "No," but then follows directions. **Most of the time acts in ways parents say are "good." May at times do things even though "knows" they are** "bad." Can follow rules if adult present. May voice some concern about badness in self and others. May ask questions about what is right and wrong.	actions approved or disapproved by parents. Much variation, depending on whether at school or at home.	questioning about what is good and what is bad.
3. Differentiating Stage: 3 to 4½ (Phallic Phase)	Knows difference between right and wrong, good and bad, as defined by his family members and their social group. Knows what kinds of behavior are approved and disapproved by adults, rewarded and punished; also which behaviors are expected of boys and which of girls, which are considered appropriate for each sex. Criticizes others or complains about them not acting appropriately. Can accept limits; can accept authority. Respects others' possessions. Can share, can take turns most of the time. Can accept and follow rules and schedules, respond to suggestions, follow directions,	Usually does not accept rules or schedules, usually resistant to and does not follow directions. Does not comply with internal representatives of external demands. Will not share, will not take turns. Difficulty handling routines and/or transitions; will not accept authority. Difficulty accepting any "demands" made on him; resistant to any suggestions. Cannot accept limits.	Preoccupied with being good. Extremely conscientious. Strict with self and with others. Extremely polite. Rigid, desperate quality in following routines, following directions, accepting suggestions. *Always* follows rules, accepts authority. Great concern about following schedules. *Must* share — often gives the other a bigger share than self. *Must* take turns — often gives the other a longer turn than self. Makes rules for others, directs them.

Phase	Characteristic, expected, typical	Uncharacteristic, unexpected, untypical, pathological Ranging from:	To:
	handle routines and transitions, though at times may need help from adult. May be "good" even though adult is not present. (Girls more strict with self than are boys, especially at school and outside the home.) Awareness of and some concern about goodness-badness in others. Criticizes "bad" children and warns other children not to be "bad."		
4. Family Integration: 4½ to 6 (Oedipal Phase)	Beginning internalization of norms; autonomous "code" of behavior. Independent capacity to decide right and wrong in many instances. Forbids self to want certain things (e.g., opposite-sex parent) and feels guilty for wishes and anticipates punishment for them. Forbids self to do certain things and feels guilty after acts. More strict with self than at earlier age (girls more so than boys).	Little capacity to decide right and wrong. Little guilt. Little internalization of norms.	Preoccupied with being "correct," acting "right." Overly severe superego; great guilt. Regards most of his actions and thoughts as "bad," feels guilty, "hates" self. Even thinking something he thinks is "bad," child feels guilty, sees self as "bad," "hates" self.

Criteria for Assessing
SUPEREGO DEVELOPMENT

Phase	Characteristic, expected, typical	Punishment Uncharacteristic, unexpected, untypical, pathological	
		Ranging from:	To:
1. Infant: birth to 1½ (Oral Phase)	Does not anticipate punishment. If punished or reprimanded, may cry, and then move on to other activities.	Punishment has little effect. May immediately return to the forbidden act.	Extreme reaction to punishment or reprimand — as if fears abandonment for being bad.
2. Toddler: 1½ to 3 (Anal Phase)	May take role of authority toward self — may scold self after doing something forbidden; may slap own hand. In play, may teach dolls or animals what is approved and disapproved. May anticipate punishment after wrongdoing and try to avoid it by blaming others (such as another child, imaginary friend, pet). May deny the act actually happened. If reprimanded, may seek affection afterwards as reassurance.	Lack of concern about punishment, lack of interest in the rules.	Terrified of doing wrong, making a mistake. Extremely fearful of punishment. Sees faults in others and has punitive attitude toward them, as well as toward self. If reprimanded, acts as if he fears the loss of love. If reprimanded, must seek reassurance afterwards.
3. Differentiating Stage: 3 to 4½ (Phallic Phase)	After wrongdoing, expects punishment. Most of the time, takes it in stride. May try to lessen punishment by promising not to act that way again. If reprimanded, may act injured; may act ashamed.	Completely unconcerned about punishment and unaffected by it.	Extreme overreaction to punishment.

Phase	Characteristic, expected, typical	Uncharacteristic, unexpected, untypical, pathological	
		Ranging from:	To:
4. Family Integration: 4½ to 6 (Oedipal Phase)	Expects punishment if breaks rules or acts in forbidden ways. If reprimanded, feels guilty. Feels guilty himself, even if no one else sees the wrongdoing, and may punish himself for what he has done or may try to atone or make amends.	Shows no guilt. No anticipation of punishment for wrongdoing. No reaction to punishment; no regret, no indication of future change in actions.	Extremely guilty. *Always* anticipates punishment, even for minor acts. *Always* affected by punishment — extremely contrite; *having* to atone and make amends. Guilt may continue for extended time after punishment.

Criteria for Assessing
SUPEREGO DEVELOPMENT

Self-Esteem

Phase	Characteristic, expected, typical	Uncharacteristic, unexpected, untypical, pathological	
		Ranging from:	To:
1. Infant:birth to 1½ (Oral Phase)	Not yet developed.		
2. Toddler: 1½ to 3 (Anal Phase)	Feels good when parent praises; feels bad when reprimanded. Enjoys being praised, admired; acts in ways to get praise, admiration. Self-feeling shifts back and forth between high and low, depending on others' evaluations. Few standards of his own. Frequent shifts in self-feelings and in confidence which is easily shaken.	Parent's praise or criticism has no effect; untouched by their opinions.	Focused on what parents will say. Most actions oriented toward getting their approval, avoiding their criticism.
3. Differentiating Stage: 3½ to 4 (Phallic Phase)	Proud of being a boy/girl; proud of body, appearance, capabilities. Feels lovable, good, worthwhile, attractive, adequate, competent. Expects to be liked by others. Positive feelings about self when "good" or acts appropriately; negative feelings when "bad" or acts inappropriately. Most of the time appears to have a good opinion of self. (Girls more likely than boys to have self-feelings influenced by others' evaluations and by the situation.)	Ashamed of being a boy/girl or of his/her body, appearance, capabilities. Feels unlovable, bad, worthless, hateful, unattractive, inadequate, incompetent. Expects not to be liked by others. Appears to have low self-esteem. Opinion of self is not good. "Inferiority feelings."	Appears grandiose, as overcompensation for low self-esteem. Acts superior — to cover up. May show extreme shifts back and forth between very high and very low self-esteem, depending on others' evaluations and on the situation.

Phase	Characteristic, expected, typical	Uncharacteristic, unexpected, untypical, pathological	
		Ranging from:	To:
4. Family Integration: 4 to 6½ (Oedipal Phase)	Achieves own standards and sees self as successful. Appears to feel self-confident, self-assured; secure about his abilities; competent. Usually proud of his own work; takes pride in doing things well. Wants to emulate ideal of parents. Idealizes and identifies with parents and wants to comply with their demands.	Usually sets standards unrealistically high. Cannot meet own standards and sees self as unsuccessful. Feels inadequate in meeting own standards, feels stupid, bad. Appears to lack self-confidence; feels insecure about own abilities; doubts self. Usually not proud of own work.	Precociously identified with parental values; acts like "small adult." Perfectionistic. Righteous about own behavior. Intolerant with others. May appear smug.

Chapter 7
Assessment of
Developmental Progression

Though each of the five aspects of development considered — social development, emotional development, ego development, phase development, and superego development — can be considered and assessed separately, and each certainly has a significant contribution to make in the overall assessment of the developmental progression of a child, the final assessment is not simply a summing up of the five. Rather, it resembles an organic integration, where the final outcome is more than the sum of the parts.

Emphasis is on a global impression of the child's development, in order to differentiate (a) between children who seem to be progressing in their development and children who seem to be having some interference with their development, and (b) between children who show minimal pathology and children whose pathology slows, or temporarily interrupts, further development.

Variations in Development

The task of assessing developmental progression is complicated by the fact that with children in the preschool-kindergarten age group, there is not just one model of development; there are, instead, many variations in development.

Some children may show a picture of overlapping phases of development, rather than neatly completing one phase of development before the next phase is systematically begun. For example, a child may show some manifestations of the oral phase, anal phase, and phallic phase, and yet primarily give evidence of being in the Oedipal phase of development.

Some children may show much fluctuation of progressive and regressive movement, so that even experienced clinicians may be unsure about what weight to give apparent fixations or regressive manifestations at a given time, while other children show little fluctuation of progressive-regressive movement. For some children, development moves forward with only a rare regression; for others, there is an ease of regression and almost a fluidity of movement.

Complicating the picture further is the fact that each child seems to have his own timetable of progression; and this has to be taken into consideration in assessing his development. With some children, development seems to proceed in slow motion for a while and then spurt forward, while for others the opposite pattern is true. Some show a slow rate of development throughout childhood, while others progress at almost breakneck speed.

For some children, there is an evenness of development in all areas during this age period; whereas for others there is unevenness, with precocity in some aspects, such as language or interpersonal relations.

Thus, in assessing a given child, it is essential to take into consideration his own pattern of development.

Meanings of Symptoms

Another complication in the task of assessing developmental progression is the finding that similar overt behavior may have different meanings for different children, and any one variable may be merely suggestive of the total picture of developmental progression. Disorders may be seen as related more to one phase of development than to another. Or, the same symptom may have many meanings. A behavior can look oral, and yet have a meaning on the anal, phallic, or Oedipal level. For example, in the case of a child with separation anxiety, it may be difficult to tell whether he is unable to separate from the mother because he is still in the oral phase, or whether he is in the Oedipal phase and unable to separate because of anxiety about his own murderous and incestuous wishes.

Any given bit of behavior can represent an intermixture of drive, ego, and superego components; and it can, therefore, be assessed in terms of each aspect of development in turn.

Prevalence of Pathology

In the extensive and comprehensive longitudinal study of nonclinical children attending community nursery schools, it was found that every child had some behaviors or symptoms that might be considered pathological to some extent. The fundamental question, therefore, was with regard to how much of the child's development and functioning had been affected by the pathology. If the child was still able to function adequately and to progress in significant areas, this would indicate that the symptom or problem was not taking up so much of the child's energies and so impairing his functioning that it interfered with developmental progression. Any symptom, conflict, pathology, disorder, had to be looked at within the context of the total picture.

Some symptoms may occur during development and eventually disappear without affecting development. Certain symptoms occur in response to the environment. They may be culturally determined and not as significant as other symptoms.

Other symptoms may be more reactive to a specific situation; a temporary adaptive response to one situation would be expected to disappear in a different situation. Other symptoms are more internalized by the child and may show continuity over many different situations and over time.

Pathology may or may not interfere with developmental progression; even if it does interfere, it may be overcome in the sense that developmental progression is again noticeable after a period of interference. Development may be interfered with for either a short or long period of time and then resumed. A child may need a shorter or longer time to recover from such events as beginning nursery school, the illness or death of a parent, the birth of a sibling, the divorce of parents, moving to a new city. Stress situations may lead to pathology and/or interference with development. The interference may occur in the current phase of the child's development or may have occurred earlier and continued for some time from a previous phase.

Thus, in assessing the child, there are two separate but major considerations: (1) whether or not there is pathology, and (2) whether development has been interfered with in significant areas or is continuing.

Recommendations for Action

Once a judgment has been made that there is pathology in significant areas, or that there is interference with development, the next step is to explore possible explanations for this finding. For example, is the observed behavior or symptom the child's reaction to a recent or current change in his situation? Or is it part of a long-continuing constellation? This should be of assistance in the next step, which is to consider various types of action that one might take with this child within the current ongoing situation. The teacher or child-care worker or community health professional who is assessing the child is also the one who makes the recommendations (to himself or herself) as to the action that seems advisable at this time. For example, some problems are best dealt with by the teacher giving the child more individual time or arranging for him to engage in certain activities. Some problems, on the other hand, may be best dealt with by removing the child from the group at school that precipitated or accentuated his problems and placing him in a new group where he may try out different and novel ways of interacting with his peers.

Other problems may be dealt with by meeting with the child's parents to discuss the situation with them and to give them an awareness of the difficulties he is having and some indication as to how the child could be helped at home or how the stresses on the child could be lessened or minimized.

The most serious or baffling problems may be dealt with by the nonclinical professional consulting with a mental health specialist who could offer advice as to certain actions to take, or who might suggest a more intensive clinical study of the child or might indicate that therapeutic help is needed and suggest a possible resource for this help.

By first becoming aware that a child's development is not progressing as would be expected, and then by reviewing the child's current situation, as well as the child's own strengths and weaknesses, alternative actions and plans for actions can be more realistically based.

Physical Health

Though physical health itself is not an aspect of development, it is included in the short assessment outline to prevent any hasty decisions about emotional problems when in actuality some physical impairment might be involved.

Another reason for including this variable, however, is because the state of a child's physical health can affect other areas of development. It will make a great difference if a child is physically healthy with no outstanding disabilities, if he has chronic physical problems or frequent illness, if he is often hospitalized, or if he has a major operation or accident. Physical handicaps or diseases can have great import on social or emotional development, as well as on ego functioning.

Another reason for looking at physical health is that disturbances in other aspects of development may be reflected in the area of physical health. Physical dysfunctioning or somatization, psychosomatic symptoms or conversion reactions, may be used as a way of coping with conflict. Thus, there may be allergies, asthma, headaches, stomachaches, frequent colds, frequent accidents, etc.

Therefore, whenever there is a sign of physical problems or a physical complaint, it is advisable that one of the recommendations of the teacher be a physical examination, in addition to whatever other recommendations are made.

Uses of Short Assessment Outline

The present version of the short assessment outline is for use by nursery school and kindergarten teachers and other professionals in the day-care and community-health fields who are in regular contact with children and can complete the form and answer the various questions on the basis of their own personal experiences with the children.

It is intended to be used flexibly by the respondent for his or her own purposes. It can assist the respondent in making explicit what he or she already knows about the child. But, in addition to this purpose, the assessment outline is designed to alert the respondent to the developmental state of a child, as well as to some of the child's problem areas.

The short assessment outline can be used as an initial screening procedure from which a gross assessment of a young child's development can be made. Thus children needing further intensive study or special attention can be singled out. Clinical people can then be brought in either for consultation or for a more complete assessment of the child. The short assessment outline is not intended to be used as a substitute for a lengthier detailed report about a child's functioning, but only as an initial "rough" assessment, suggesting directions for further action.

The short assessment outline may also be used to make comparisons of a child at different times. By filling it out at the beginning of the year and again at the end of the year, it is possible to see whether a child is showing continuing

progression in development or some interference, and to
see in which areas of development changes have taken
place. On the other hand, a teacher may just want to use it
near the beginning of a semester as a basis for planning a
program for the child's activities; or just at the end of the
year as a summary statement about the child, for use by
others who may have future contact with him.

In our contacts with educational and training institutions, we have found that the short assessment outline
can also be used as a teaching device in college un-
dergraduate or graduate classes concerned with child
development, or in in-service training programs with
professionals and paraprofessionals. The outline may
provide such persons with new information about early
child development and with new ways of looking at
children — from a different point of view. It may even
suggest ways in which a nonclinician can have a role in
modifying the child's environment.

Nonclinical persons who are asked to make judgments
about certain aspects of development must perforce
observe children more closely. As a consequence, such
persons may achieve a new orientation and a sharpened
perception that may enable them to note behaviors they
had previously not seen; or they may become more aware
of situations that call for giving a child some type of special
attention. In addition, they may begin to recognize the
hitherto overlooked problems of the child or may become
aware of some of the ways the young child uses his
environment. This, in turn, may affect the teacher's own
interactions with the children and can guide her in
planning certain actions with the children.

It has long been recognized that, at this early age, the
child's environment is of great importance to his development and that, because of their continuing and pervasive
influence on the child, the parents are the principal part of
this environment. They can support or fail to support ego
strength; they can act as models for identification; they can
reinforce regressive moves; they can overgratify certain
drives. The short assessment outline can also be used as a

basis for conferences between teachers and parents — to indicate to the parents the problem areas of the child, to suggest to the parents more effective ways of handling the child, or to point out to them some of the effects on the child of the parents' behaviors.

Appendix A
Reduction to the
Essential Features

To obtain items for the short version of the *Assessment Outline of Early Child Development,* three different analyses were undertaken of the data gathered in the research done with the samples of nonclinical children attending community nursery schools. First, the research staff did an intensive content analysis of the dynamic summaries that had been written by the clinicians in the course of making their assessments of the children. This analysis was for the purpose of determining which aspects of development, as well as which specific behaviors or characteristics within each aspect, were emphasized or mentioned as a basis for assessing the given child. From such a content analysis, it was possible to discover those aspects or behaviors the clinicians themselves indicated as being important bases for their final judgments in evaluating the children.

Second, an extensive outline of items of behavior and aspects of development was prepared, based on the recorded interviews with parents, teachers, and children — and on the observations that had been done in the school setting. Then, for each child who had been studied, the clinician who had done the interviewing and observing evaluated (on a five-point scale) each of the items with regard to how significant it had been to him in arriving at his final assessment of the child. Despite individual response tendencies among the clinicians, certain items stood out as being regarded by the clinicians as more significant than other items.

Third, a comprehensive outline of behaviors and aspects of development was presented to research staff members who had not studied the children. These staff members first filled in the outline for each child on the basis of just reading the recorded interviews and observations, and then made a judgment about the child's grouping from the outline. This process showed what kinds of information could be obtained from the interviews and observations, as well as which items were associated with different groupings of children.

Following these three types of analyses, certain items were eliminated where there was no difference between the groupings of the children with regard to the given item. For example, one item referred to "memory." Almost every child in the research study was described by a parent or a teacher as having a good memory. Therefore, this item was omitted in the final short version of the *Assessment Outline of Early Child Development.*

Items were also eliminated from the outline if the clinicians indicated that the items were of little or no significance in making an assessment of the child's developmental progression.

In addition, items were eliminated where there was insufficient information from the interviews or the observations to be able to make a judgment about the item for many of the children. For example, it was desirable to look at the child's capacity to differentiate between fantasy and reality. But, when questions were asked of the parents and teachers about the child's fantasies, they could not give answers to provide the necessary information to enable the clinicians to make evaluations of the child. Rather, this type of information was more accessible and more easily evaluated on the psychological tests.

Criteria for Outline

Several criteria were specifically set forth as guidelines for the final version of the *Assessment Outline of Early Child Development*. One criterion was that only those aspects of development shown by the investigation to be *most significant as indicators* of developmental progression, and/or pathology, were to be included. The assessment of the nonclinical children by the clinicians in the research study had been a much more sophisticated and extensive process than was needed by or useful to nonclinicians. However, from such an extensive and intensive investigation as was done, it was possible to determine what was important for nonclinicians to look at in order to differentiate between children showing developmental progression and children showing interference with development in significant areas, as well as to become aware of children with pathology.

Another criterion was that the short version of the *Assessment Outline of Early Child Development* was to be limited to the *minimum material necessary*. Since only a gross assessment of a young child's development was to be made, it was preferable to include only a small number of essential items rather than to require a full statement about the development of a child. The goal was to develop an outline that could be filled out in twenty or thirty minutes — a great reduction from the twenty-five hours that had been required for a complete clinical work-up and assessment on each child each year of the research study.

A third criterion was that there was to be *concentration on those aspects of development and items of behavior most accessible to nonclinicians and most useful to them*, in terms of their own contacts with young children. This meant including the kinds of behaviors usually mentioned by teachers in their interviews and eliminating items that referred to the unconscious or items that required high-level, inductive reasoning or interpretation by clinicians.

In addition, it was decided that all items were to be *stated in a simple, unambiguous, and direct way, and in language relevant to nonclinicians* who would ultimately be using this short version of the *Assessment Outline of Early Child Development.*

Format for Outline

Various formats were tried before arriving at the final one for the *Assessment Outline of Early Child Development.* The first used open-ended questions similar to the type that had been used for the interviews with parents and teachers. However, nonclinical professionals who filled these out objected that the task took too long and felt tedious. On the other hand, when just multiple choice items were presented, the respondents objected that this did not do justice to some children because the respondents felt they had to "squeeze" children into the alternatives presented. The final format, therefore, presents a rating system for the various items along with space for comments about the individual child and instructions that encourage the respondents to mark the outline flexibly, keeping in mind how the respondent plans to use the results of the assessment.

Preliminary Trials

The *Assessment Outline of Early Child Development* was first tried out with teachers who had been participating in the ongoing research projects. They had already been interviewed by the staff clinicians and were acquainted with the kinds of information being sought about the nonclinical children.

In addition, the Outline was tried with a group of teachers in the prekindergarten group of the public school system in New York City, and with some of the teachers in the therapeutic nursery school at the Child Development Center.

All of the teachers who participated assisted the project by criticizing the various formats that were tried, criticizing the language and emphasizing the need to simplify the wording, suggesting words for the rating scales, and even suggesting the use of different colored paper for different sections of the *Assessment Outline of Early Child Development.*

Appendix B
Validity and Reliability

The item selection for the *Assessment Outline of Early Child Development* determined that the type of information gathered followed the theoretical formulations on which the study was based; thus, there was content validity. However, in order to make sure that as a result of the many changes in format and in the wording of items, information was not lost and that the final version did not bias assessment, other analyses were carried out.

In making comparisons of the different assessments, three types of agreement were distinguished:

1. *Agreement about developmental progression.* The groupings by nonclinicians and the groupings by clinicians agreed that developmental progression had or had not been maintained, disregarding pathology. That is, both believed that the given child belonged in either Group 1a (Progression in development has been maintained as would be expected) or Group 1b (Progression in development has been maintained, but with significant accompanying pathological features).

2. *Agreement about pathology.* The groupings by nonclinicians and the groupings by clinicians agreed that pathology existed, disregarding progression in development. That is, both believed that the given child belonged in either Group 1b (Progression in

development has been maintained, but with significant accompanying pathological features) or Group 2 (Development has been interfered with in significant areas).

3. *Complete agreement.* The groupings by nonclinicians and the groupings by clinicians agreed that developmental progression had or had not been maintained *and* agreed that significant pathology did or did not occur. That is, both believed that the given child belonged in the same group.

It had been found previously in studying the sample of nonclinical children from a community nursery school that, in comparing the overall development assessments based on an integration of all information by the clinicians with the assessments based on only the teacher interviews, there was 72% agreement for the boys and 71% agreement for the girls. Thus, the information from the teacher interviews alone could give a fairly accurate preliminary assessment of the child's developmental progression.

The evaluations of the children made by teachers who filled out the *Assessment Outline of Early Child Development* were then compared with the evaluations of the children made by clinicians integrating all the information from all sources — interviews with parents, teachers, and children; observations of the children in the school setting; and psychological tests.

With regard to whether or not developmental progression had been maintained, teachers using the *Assessment Outline of Early Child Development* and clinicians using an integration of all information available, agreed on 93% of the children; while with regard to whether or not significant pathology was present, the teachers and clinicians agreed on 80% of the children. There was agreement on both developmental progression and significant pathology — that is, complete agreement — on 73% of the children. Thus, the agreement between assessments of children based on the clinicians' integration of all information available and assessments of children based on the teachers' use of the *Assessment Outline of Early Child*

Development was as good as the agreement had been between assessments based on the clinicians' integration of all information available and assessments based on the clinical interviews with teachers.

The second type of analysis was made by having a group of clinicians who did *not* do the original interviewing read the clinical interviews with teachers and fill out the *Assessment Outline of Early Child Development* on the basis of the information in the recorded interview. Following this, another group of clinicians — who had neither conducted the interviews nor read the report of the clinical interviews — assessed the children only on the basis of reading the filled-out *Assessment Outline of Early Child Development* for each child. With regard to whether or not developmental progression had been maintained, clinicians who assessed the children from the *Assessment Outline of Early Child Development* and clinicians who assessed the children by using an integration of all information available, agreed on 93% of the children; while with regard to whether or not significant pathology was present, they agreed on 87% of the children. There was agreement on both developmental progression and significant pathology on 80% of the children.

Comparisons of Descriptions

There was some question as to how the information given by the *Assessment Outline of Early Child Development* compared with the specific information obtained in the interview and observational material. Therefore a group of clinicians who had available and read only the filled-out *Assessment Outline of Early Child Development* were asked to write short descriptive statements about each child, based on this information alone. The descriptive statements were to be written in a style similar to that used by the original clinicians in justifying and giving the reasons for their assessments and briefly describing the child in the dynamic summaries. This would indicate whether the items in the *Assessment Outline of Early*

Child Development give enough data to describe the children in statements similar to those in the interview and observational material.

To answer this question, the brief descriptions written by the clinicians who did the initial interviewing and wrote dynamic summaries of the material were compared with the brief descriptions written by the clinicians who had available only the responses on the *Assessment Outline of Early Child Development* as information about the children. Similarities in the content of these descriptions were quite striking concerning the discussions of social development, emotional development, ego development, phase development, and superego development.

The findings indicate that the information given by the *Assessment Outline of Early Child Development* is of a type that allows nonclinicians to make assessments of children similar to the assessments made by clinicians. The findings also indicate that the specific information available in the responses to the *Assessment Outline of Early Child Development* can be used as a basis to make descriptive statements about a child similar to the types of statements that might be found in a dynamic summary of clinical interviews with the child, his parents, and his teachers.

Some differences did, however, appear in the content of the clinical interviews and the content of the *Assessment Outline of Early Child Development*. The teacher-interview-based descriptions of the child's social development are somewhat more detailed than are the descriptions in the *Assessment Outline of Early Child Development*. On the other hand, the *Assessment Outline of Early Child Development* emphasized a bit more the developmental characteristics of a child than did the interview descriptions.

Another difference was that the internal environment of the child, such as his needs and motivations, were discussed in more detail in the teacher-interview-based descriptions than in the *Assessment Outline of Early Child Development*. This may be due to the fact that in the interviews, the clinicians could probe more and follow up any questions they had about a specific response of the teacher.

Finally, the impression of the clinician as to the accuracy of the teachers' responses was usually mentioned in the interview-based descriptions, whereas this was not possible to evaluate when teachers used the *Assessment Outline of Early Child Development.*

ASSESSMENT OUTLINE OF EARLY CHILD DEVELOPMENT*

by Dorothy Flapan, Ph.D.
and Peter B. Neubauer, M.D.[1]

This Assessment Outline is designed as a guide to help you formulate and make explicit what you know about a given child. It permits the study of the child's progression or lack of progression in development and points out the specific factors that are important in his development. It does not lead to a clinical diagnostic statement, but it can be used as an adjunct by providing the developmental components of the child's deviation.

The Outline is to be filled out on the basis of your direct experience with the child rather than on the basis of information you have about the child from other sources. It can be filled out after even a brief period of contact with a child. As with any guide, however, it is unlikely that all you want to record about a specific child will be included. To enhance its usefulness, we suggest that, for your own purposes, you may want to reformulate a statement or add statements that are not included in the Outline.

*Copyright, July 1974, New York City.
[1] Mr. Ruediger Schroeer helped in devising this version of the Short Assessment Outline and in determining validity and reliability.

Based on your responses to the items in the Outline, as well as whatever comments you have made in the spaces provided, you can proceed (on page 14) to make a final assessment of the child and to indicate (on page 15) the kinds of problems that you think the child has; and this, in turn will lead to your recommendations for dealing with these problems (also on page 16).

The form usually requires 20–30 minutes to fill out. It is not intended to be used as a substitute for a lengthier, more intensive report, but as an initial assessment, suggesting possible directions for action. We found it to be useful to have the Assessment Outline filled out at various times during the year in order to evaluate changes. It may also be used as a year-end summary or as a report for others who will have contacts with the child or as a means for conferring with the child's parents.

IDENTIFYING DATA

Child's Name _____ Date _____

Age _____ Sex _____ Birth Position _____ Number of Siblings _____

Education of Father _____ Education of Mother _____

Occupation of Father _____ Occupation of Mother _____

Length of Time in School _____ Length of Time in Group _____

Previous Test Records:

Other Pertinent Information About the Child:

Directions for Page 4

On page 4 you will find nine items that deal with the development of various abilities. Indicate how this child compares with other children the same age by circling the appropriate number.

Circling (1) indicates that on the given item this child seems like children *much younger* than his chronological age.

Circling (2) indicates that on the given item this child seems like children *somewhat younger* than his chronological age.

Circling (3) indicates that on the given item this child seems about *average* for his chronological age.

Circling (4) indicates that on the given item this child seems *above average* for his chronological age.

In addition, in order to individualize your assessment of this child, in the column on the right you may record:

    (a)   recent changes
    (b)   conditions under which the ability varies
    (c)   how the ability is manifested
    (d)   any other comments

Hypothetical example:

Item	Comparison with others the same chronological age	Recent changes, conditions under which the ability varies, how the ability is manifested, any other comments
Ability to deal with difficult or new situations	1 ② 3 4	Has recently become worse. Handles some new situations adequately, but often withdraws or retreats inappropriately when a stranger comes into the room.

In this hypothetical example, the respondent has indicated that this child's ability to deal with difficult or lessened.

Item	Comparison with others the same chronological age			Recent changes, conditions under which the ability varies, how the ability is manifested, any other comments
Coordination of large body movement	1	2 3	4	
Coordination of small body movement (dexterity)	1	2 3	4	
Vocabulary	1	2 3	4	
Verbal communication with adults	1	2 3	4	
Verbal communication with children	1	2 3	4	
Ability to use various materials	1	2 3	4	
Ability to deal with difficult or new situations	1	2 3	4	
Ability to wait and/or take turns	1	2 3	4	
Ability to pay attention and to concentrate	1	2 3	4	
Curiosity, interest in exploring and learning	1	2 3	4	

(1) Like children much younger than his chronological age
(2) Like children somewhat younger than his chronological age
(3) About average for his chronological age
(4) Above average for chronological age

On pages 6 and 7 you will find items that deal with affection, aggression, and mood, as well as items that are labeled "miscellaneous." Indicate how often the child shows the various qualities of behaviors or emotions by circling the appropriate number for each.

Indicate that this child shows the particular quality of behavior or emotion by circling
(0) Not at all   (1) Rarely   (2) Some of the time   (3) Most of the time

(If you cannot respond to a specific item, leave it blank until you have further information. Often there is not enough information available about the child's interaction with a parent, and it is only after a period of sensitive observation that the item can be marked.)

In addition, in order to individualize your assessment of this child, in the column on the right you may record:
(a) recent changes
(b) circumstances that stimulate the specific quality of behavior and/or emotion
(c) whether emotions felt are directly expressed or are covered up
(d) how the feelings are expressed
(e) any other comments

Hypothetical example:

Item	Qualities of Behaviors or Emotions				Recent changes, circumstances that stimulate the specific quality of behavior and/or emotion, whether emotions felt are directly expressed or are covered up, how the feelings are expressed, any other comments
	extreme, intense	artificial, exaggerated, overdemonstrative	very controlled or inhibited	open, direct spontaneous	
Expression of affection with					
mother	⓪ 1 2 3	⓪ 1 2 3	0 1 2 ③	0 ① 2 3	This has been a problem of long standing. Once in a while he may briefly hold another child's hand.
father	⓪ 1 2 3	⓪ 1 2 3	0 1 2 ③	0 ① 2 3	
teacher	⓪ 1 2 3	⓪ 1 2 3	0 1 2 ③	0 ① 2 3	
children	⓪ 1 2 3	⓪ 1 2 3	0 1 2 ③	0 1 ② 3	

In this hypothetical example, the respondent has indicated that most of the time this child is very controlled or inhibited in his expression of affection with mother, father, teacher, and children. Sometimes the child can spontaneously express affection with children. This is a problem of long standing.

Qualities of Behaviors or Emotions

Item					Recent changes, circumstances which stimulate the specific quality of behavior and/or emotion, whether emotions felt are directly expressed or are covered up, how the feelings are expressed, any other comments.
Expression of affection with	extreme, intense	artificial, exaggerated, overdemonstrative	very controlled or inhibited	open, direct spontaneous	
mother	0 1 2 3	0 1 2 3	0 1 2 3	0 1 2 3	
father	0 1 2 3	0 1 2 3	0 1 2 3	0 1 2 3	
teacher	0 1 2 3	0 1 2 3	0 1 2 3	0 1 2 3	
children	0 1 2 3	0 1 2 3	0 1 2 3	0 1 2 3	
Response to expression of affection from	shows strong need for it	anxious, uncomfortable	ignores, acts uninterested	accepts easily, pleased, responsive	
mother	0 1 2 3	0 1 2 3	0 1 2 3	0 1 2 3	
father	0 1 2 3	0 1 2 3	0 1 2 3	0 1 2 3	
teacher	0 1 2 3	0 1 2 3	0 1 2 3	0 1 2 3	
children	0 1 2 3	0 1 2 3	0 1 2 3	0 1 2 3	
Expression of aggression toward	extreme, intense	artificial, exaggerated, caricatured	very controlled or inhibited	moderate, direct, spontaneous	
mother	0 1 2 3	0 1 2 3	0 1 2 3	0 1 2 3	
father	0 1 2 3	0 1 2 3	0 1 2 3	0 1 2 3	
teacher	0 1 2 3	0 1 2 3	0 1 2 3	0 1 2 3	
children	0 1 2 3	0 1 2 3	0 1 2 3	0 1 2 3	
Response to reprimands of	extreme aggression	anxiety, withdrawal	seems to ignore, not notice	tolerates, responds moderately	
mother	0 1 2 3	0 1 2 3	0 1 2 3	0 1 2 3	
father	0 1 2 3	0 1 2 3	0 1 2 3	0 1 2 3	
teacher	0 1 2 3	0 1 2 3	0 1 2 3	0 1 2 3	

(0) Not at all   (2) Some of the time
(1) Rarely   (3) Most of the time

Qualities of Behaviors or Emotions

Item					Recent changes, circumstances which stimulate the specific quality of behavior and/or emotion, whether emotions felt are directly expressed or are covered up, how the feelings are expressed, any other comments
Response to expression of aggression by children	extreme aggression 0 1 2 3	anxiety, withdrawal 0 1 2 3	seems to ignore, not notice 0 1 2 3	tolerates, responds moderately 0 1 2 3	
Characteristic mood	angry, annoyed 0 1 2 3	anxious, fearful 0 1 2 3	sad, unhappy 0 1 2 3	happy, contented 0 1 2 3	

Miscellaneous

Item	Characteristic Descriptions				Recent changes, circumstances that stimulate the specific behavior, any other comments
Body activity	rigid, stiff 0 1 2 3	slow, cautious 0 1 2 3	wild and/or uncontrolled 0 1 2 3	free and spontaneous 0 1 2 3	
Social interaction	alone 0 1 2 3	with teacher 0 1 2 3	with one child 0 1 2 3	with group of children 0 1 2 3	
Quality of play	solitary 0 1 2 3	parallel and/or imitative 0 1 2 3	competitive, challenging 0 1 2 3	cooperative 0 1 2 3	

(0) Not at all   (2) Some of the time
(1) Rarely   (3) Most of the time

Directions for Pages 9, 10, and 11

On pages 9, 10, and 11 you will find items that outline developmental characteristics and social relationships. Indicate how often the child shows the characteristic or behavior by circling the appropriate number for each.

Circling (0) indicates that the characteristic or behavior is observed *not at all.*
Circling (1) indicates that the characteristic or behavior is observed *rarely.*
Circling (2) indicates that the characteristic or behavior is observed *some of the time.*
Circling (3) indicates that the characteristic or behavior is observed *most of the time.*

(If you cannot respond to a specific item, leave it blank until you have further information. Often there is not enough information available about the child's interaction with a parent; and it is only after a period of sensitive observation that the item can be marked.)

In addition, in order to individualize your assessment of this child, in the column on the right you may record:

(a) recent changes
(b) circumstances which stimulate the characteristic or behavior
(c) how the characteristic or behavior is shown
(d) a phrase that better describes the child
(e) any other comments

Hypothetical example:

Characteristic	Father	Mother	Teacher	Boys	Girls	Recent changes, circumstances that stimulate the characteristic or behavior, how the characteristic or behavior is shown, a phrase that better describes the child, any other comments.
Complains to, whines when with	0 1 2 ③	0 1 2 ③	0 1 2 ③	0 ① 2 3	0 1 ② 3	Complains to parents about what other children have that he does not have; to teacher that other children have wronged him; to girls when he feels they are not playing fair. Less complaining recently.

In this hypothetical example, the respondent has indicated that most of the complaining is to adults and some is to girls; but there is rarely any complaining to boys. There has been improvement recently.

Characteristic	Father	Mother	Teacher	Boys	Girls	Recent changes, circumstances which stimulate the characteristic or behavior, how the characteristic or behavior is shown, a phrase that better describes the child, any other comments.
Obedient, compliant with	0 1 2 3	0 1 2 3	0 1 2 3	0 1 2 3	0 1 2 3	
Clings to	0 1 2 3	0 1 2 3	0 1 2 3	0 1 2 3	0 1 2 3	
Apathetic, withdrawn with	0 1 2 3	0 1 2 3	0 1 2 3	0 1 2 3	0 1 2 3	
Dependent on	0 1 2 3	0 1 2 3	0 1 2 3	0 1 2 3	0 1 2 3	
Demanding with	0 1 2 3	0 1 2 3	0 1 2 3	0 1 2 3	0 1 2 3	
Complains to, whines when with	0 1 2 3	0 1 2 3	0 1 2 3	0 1 2 3	0 1 2 3	
Asks for help from	0 1 2 3	0 1 2 3	0 1 2 3	0 1 2 3	0 1 2 3	
Negative, defiant to	0 1 2 3	0 1 2 3	0 1 2 3	0 1 2 3	0 1 2 3	
Stubborn toward	0 1 2 3	0 1 2 3	0 1 2 3	0 1 2 3	0 1 2 3	
Bossy, domineering with	0 1 2 3	0 1 2 3	0 1 2 3	0 1 2 3	0 1 2 3	

(0) Not at all   (2) Some of the time
(1) Rarely   (3) Most of the time

Characteristic	Father	Mother	Teacher	Boys	Girls	Recent changes, circumstances which stimulate the characteristic or behavior, how the characteristic or behavior is shown, a phrase that better describes the child, any other comments.
Friendly, cooperative with	0 1 2 3	0 1 2 3	0 1 2 3	0 1 2 3	0 1 2 3	
Competitive, bragging, challenging with	0 1 2 3	0 1 2 3	0 1 2 3	0 1 2 3	0 1 2 3	
Assertive, forceful with	0 1 2 3	0 1 2 3	0 1 2 3	0 1 2 3	0 1 2 3	
Passive, unassertive with	0 1 2 3	0 1 2 3	0 1 2 3	0 1 2 3	0 1 2 3	
Actively seeks attention of	0 1 2 3	0 1 2 3	0 1 2 3	0 1 2 3	0 1 2 3	
Avoids attention of	0 1 2 3	0 1 2 3	0 1 2 3	0 1 2 3	0 1 2 3	
Shows off to	0 1 2 3	0 1 2 3	0 1 2 3	0 1 2 3	0 1 2 3	
Seductive, manipulating with	0 1 2 3	0 1 2 3	0 1 2 3	0 1 2 3	0 1 2 3	
Shows concern and sympathy for	0 1 2 3	0 1 2 3	0 1 2 3	0 1 2 3	0 1 2 3	
Aware of and responsive to the needs and feelings of	0 1 2 3	0 1 2 3	0 1 2 3	0 1 2 3	0 1 2 3	

(0) Not at all
(1) Rarely
(2) Some of the time
(3) Most of the time

Characteristic	Frequency	Recent changes, circumstances which stimulate the characteristic or behavior, how the characteristic or behavior is shown, a phrase that better describes the child, any other comments.
Gets hurt by other children	0 1 2 3	
Hurts other children	0 1 2 3	
Hurts self	0 1 2 3	
Is organized, orderly	0 1 2 3	
Is disorganized, disorderly	0 1 2 3	
Admires self, proud of self	0 1 2 3	
Admires others	0 1 2 3	
Criticizes self, finds fault with self	0 1 2 3	
Criticizes others, finds fault with others	0 1 2 3	
Expresses or shows guilt; anticipates punishment	0 1 2 3	

(0) Not at all   (2) Some of the time
(1) Rarely   (3) Most of the time

HEALTH

Check those boxes and answer the questions that apply to this child

General Health:	Poor	Fair	Good	Excellent		Describe any problems:
Hearing:	Poor	Fair	Good			Describe any problems:
		Not checked within last six months	Checked within last six months			
Eyesight:	Poor	Fair	Good			Describe any problems:
		Not checked within last six months	Checked within last six months			
Speech Impediments:	Yes, and interfere with communication	Yes, but do not interfere with communication	NO			Describe speech impediments:
Other Handicaps:	Yes, and interfere with functioning	Yes, but do not interfere with functioning	NO			Describe handicaps:

Does this child have any symptoms or difficulties that you consider to be significant? (e.g. spitting, biting, excessive thumb-sucking, eating difficulties, inappropriate fears for his age, difficulties in toilet training, excessive daydreaming, separation difficulties, etc.) Yes _____ No _____ Describe the symptoms or difficulties:

Your concerns about this child:
(You may include here reference to the child's family or life situation, as well as the development of the child.)

Strengths of this child:
(You may want to include the child's intelligence, learning capacity, adaptive functioning or other aspects of his personality which are not covered in this Assessment Outline but which you consider significant.)

Specific areas which need further investigation and clarification:

A. *Final Assessment*

Circle either 1, 2, 3, or 4 to indicate which best expresses your opinion.

(It may be difficult to decide whether to put a child into group 2 or group 3, and this in itself is an important statement.)

1. *This child is able to progress developmentally.*

   He is within the expected range for his age and sex. His functioning would be considered age adequate. No special help or attention is necessary.

2. *This child is progressing developmentally though he has problems in some areas.*

   He has conflicts and difficulties which are beyond the norm. (Certain symptoms occur in response to the environment and are not as significant as other symptoms. Therefore, any symptom is to be looked at within the total picture of developmental progression.)

3. *This child's development is not progressing appropriately.*

   There are problems that interfere with development in significant areas. (Such problems might include still depending on mother and being unable to move away from her toward other people; showing hyperactivity or impulsivity without appropriate controls; having serious learning difficulties; showing difficulty in expressing feelings; etc.)

4. *This child had problems that had interfered with his developmental progression but is currently showing improvement.*

   This is based on a recent change in the child in the direction of overcoming a symptom or coping with problems. It includes even children who are slowly starting to change; it is the change that is significant. The child might be recovering from a traumatic event, such as the illness of a parent, the birth of a sibling, change of residence, etc. Because of the trauma, there may have been some inhibition or regression before the development began moving forward again.

B. *Possible Explanations for 2, 3, or 4.*
Of the following explanations, circle as many numbers as you feel are necessary; and if you circle #1, underline all the phrases which you think are possibilities.

1. *These problems are probably a reaction to a recent or current situation.*

   e.g., Starting nursery-school, separation of parents, death of a significant person, illness of a family member or other significant person, birth of a sibling, change of residency, trip.
   Other _____

2. *These problems are probably a direct consequence of the particular group the child is in at school.*

3. *These problems are part of the child's general behavior pattern.*

4. *These problems are due to* _____

C. *Recommendations for action.*
Circle as many numbers as necessary.

1. *Help within the educational setting.* Providing special consideration for the child, such as the teacher giving him more individual time, arranging for him to engage in special activities, providing more opportunities for contact with specific other children, assisting in impulse control, assisting in developing motor skills, assisting in the separation process, or in other ways providing a corrective experience within the educational setting.

2. *Parental guidance.* Discussing the child's problems with the parent(s) in the hope that by giving the parent(s) an awareness of the child's difficulties, the parent(s) would then be able to act in a way to help the child or to minimize the problems. Specific goals with parents _____

3. *Changing the educational setting.* Putting the child into a different group at school in the hope that moving him from a group that precipitated or accentuated the problem would in itself be therapeutic.

4. *Consulting with a mental health professional* to discuss and evaluate the child's behavior.

5. *Referring the child to a mental health resource for treatment.*

6. *Deciding that no special action is necessary* in the expectation that the problem is transitory and will disappear in the natural course of development.

7. *Other* (e.g., physical check-up, speech therapy, dance therapy, art therapy, special attention to physical handicaps, etc.)

CONTINUOUS RECORD

Date	Grouping of Child (Group 1, 2, 3, 4)	Items or areas that have not changed and continue to be significant	Items or areas that have changed

INDEX